STEP IT OUT

STEP IT OUT

The 30-Day Walking
and Weight-Loss Workout

Maggie Humphreys and
Les Snowdon

Aurum Press

If you are unfit, pregnant, or have a diagnosed medical problem that will affect your ability to exercise, you should check with your doctor before commencing a vigorous exercise programme. The authors and publishers cannot accept responsibility for any injury or damage suffered as a result of attempting an exercise in this book.

First published in Great Britain
2002 by Aurum Press Ltd
25 Bedford Avenue, London WC1B 3AT

The authors would like to thank Sandra Masters, Fitness and Exercise Certificate, SKFA, for the exercise routines.

A catalogue record for this book is available from the British Library.

ISBN 1 85410 825 5

10 9 8 7 6 5 4 3 2 1
2006 2005 2004 2003 2002

Designed and typeset by M Rules
Illustrations by See Illustration
Printed and bound in Great Britain by
MPG Books Ltd, Bodmin

Contents

'Few people know how to take a walk'
Ralph Waldo Emerson

*'If everyone were to walk briskly 30 minutes a day,
we could cut the incidence of many chronic
diseases 30 to 40 per cent'*
Dr JoAnn Manson, chief of preventive medicine,
Brigham and Women's Hospital, Harvard University

Introduction

Maggie's Story

Tired, lethargic, unfit, overweight, overstressed. Recognise any of these symptoms? I certainly do.

About 12 years ago, I suddenly realised I was beginning to slow down. I was unfit, I didn't have as much energy as I used to, and I'd put on weight. At one time, I played tennis, squash and badminton regularly, and as a busy teacher, I considered myself a fairly active person. But the passing years were starting to take their toll. I found it hard to include exercise in a busy life and very easy to find excuses not to bother. I'm sure you know them all: not enough time; too tired at the end of the day; preferring to relax rather than exercise.

So I decided to exercise more and get fit. I installed an exercise bike in the bedroom. I tried following umpteen exercise plans from women's magazines. And I must have tried every exercise fad going, from going to the gym to yoga, callanetics, skipping, aqua-aerobics and jogging (oh, my poor knees!). You name it: I tried it. Not that there's anything wrong with any of these exercises – but how many people do you know who keep them up, week in, week out throughout the year?

I was desperate for something that actually worked, something that I could keep up, and something that was *fun*! And then it dawned upon me. Why not walk more often? I'd always loved walking, ever since I was a child. So I decided to step up my pace, leave the car behind a bit more often, and just get out in the fresh air. And it was a revelation.

The first thing you discover is that you don't have to spend hours in the gym to get fit. Getting fit and keeping fit can be as simple as walking out of your own front door. All you have to do is step out at a brisker pace and step out more often. That's what I did – and I'm still doing it!

Walking is simple and fun and it's the most natural exercise in the world. After all, you've been doing it since you were about a year old. It's safe and almost injury-free. And regular fitness walking does more than keep you fit: it provides a marvellous feel-good factor. It's also inexpensive – all you need is a pair of comfortable walking shoes.

And it's important for all of us, because recent statistics show that, in Britain:

- more than half the nation's adults are overweight
- up to 20 per cent are obese (at least 20 per cent above optimum body weight)

In order to be healthy, we need to exercise more and we need to be fit. Surveys repeatedly show that it's not the passing years that are a problem, it's a passive lifestyle. As technology has increasingly taken the physical effort out of our daily lives, we have become more and more inactive. Our bodies aren't meant to spend so much time sitting staring at a computer screen, slumped in front of the television, or slouched behind the wheel of a car. And even children are not far behind in the inactivity stakes.

As a teacher, I have observed over the past ten years or so that children are becoming less and less fit. I have always thought of children as being naturally fit and full of energy (they have almost too much energy at times!). But I began to notice kids being puffed out after climbing a couple of flights of stairs, kids flagging after a short time in P.E. lessons, kids standing around idly during break times, and kids finding it difficult to walk uphill on the way to school. The statistics say it all:

- by the age of 11, a third of children are overweight, with 27 per cent of boys and 13 per cent of girls classified as obese

- many children exercise less than the equivalent of one ten-minute brisk walk a week

Yet surveys suggest that children are not eating much more than they did 20 to 30 years ago. So the key difference must be – you've guessed it – exercise!

The combined effects of a poor diet and a couch-potato lifestyle, with television and computers being used as 'electronic babysitters', mean that even the slightest exertion often seems very demanding to children. Recently, I arranged a lunchtime walk and picnic on the common about five minutes' walk from the school where I was teaching. The children were really looking forward to their walk on the common, but one of them asked, 'How are we going to get there?' And then there's the perennial problem of kids being taxied around by their parents on the school run and to maintain their social life. No wonder kids are getting fatter and lazier!

So what's the answer? Well, I'm not suggesting that walking alone will solve all these problems. But it's a start. We can all walk more often. We can leave the car behind and club together to walk our kids to school when it's convenient; this would also reduce pollution and road congestion. We can walk to the shops, or park the car further away and walk from there. We can get off the bus or train a stop earlier and walk the rest of the way. There are endless ways to improvise so that we walk more every day.

In order to wake up in the morning feeling bright, energetic and confident, we need an alert mind and a fit body, and the easiest and quickest way to achieve this is to take a regular brisk walk. Walking is the easiest way for all the family to keep fit, because everyone can do it, it's cheap, and it's non-competitive. Walking also means that you spend more time together, a regular period of time when you can get fit, lose weight and . . . talk. Yes, talk! How many times have I heard parents say: 'We never seem to have time to talk these days.' So why not give walking a try?

Almost anyone can walk to keep fit. Whether you're young or old, single or married, already fairly active or have been inactive for years, whether you have a figure like Kate Moss or are 40 pounds overweight, everyone can reap the amazing benefits of walking – right now! If you follow our 30-Day Walking and Weight-Loss Workout, you will gain all-round stamina, strength and suppleness. And you will feel better, have more energy, and have the get-up-and-go to get you through each and every day.

Don't forget that healthy eating is as important as regular exercise. By combining fitness walking with our 30-Day Healthy Eating Plan, you will soon begin to shed several pounds a week and your diet will be much healthier.

I have always loved everything to do with food: choosing foods in shops and markets, cooking and, not least, eating! I particularly enjoy cooking for family and friends, and there is no way I would want to follow an eating plan that concentrates on cutting out foods; I prefer one where the emphasis is on eating delicious, fresh foods.

So I began to adapt my favourite recipes to healthier, lighter versions. Once I had started to combine fitness walking with a balanced, nutritious eating plan, I soon found that I was losing those unwanted pounds; I also felt fitter and healthier and had more energy. Research shows that people who combine healthy eating with regular moderate exercise like fitness walking are more likely to keep weight off in the long run.

Turn now to page 16 and work out which fitness level is suitable for you. Then put on a pair of comfortable shoes and step out for an exhilarating brisk walk. It may change your life forever!

STEP
ONE

It's Good to Walk

Today, exercise physiologists, cardiologists, obesity experts and stress experts all recommend walking as the best exercise for most people to get fit, lose weight and maintain long-term health. Modern science now confirms what Hippocrates, the founding father of the medical profession, said 2500 years ago: 'Walking is the best medicine.'

Whether you're young or old, walking is an easy, convenient way to get fit and stay fit. As we all walk anyway in our everyday lives, it's the obvious place to begin a fitness programme. It's just a question of walking more often and at a pace that gives you an aerobic workout.

Brisk walking at an aerobic level gives you a workout comparable to jogging, with less chance of injury. Biomechanical studies show that your feet pound the ground with more than three times your body weight when jogging, but only one to one-and-a-half times your body weight when you walk, making it the safest form of aerobic exercise around. To save any confusion, throughout the rest of this book we will refer to aerobic walking as 'fitness walking'.

A fitness walking pace for most people is a speed of around 3½ to 4 miles per hour, kept up for 20–30 minutes, at a level of intensity which leaves you slightly breathless at the end. We will explain in the next chapter how to gauge walking speed and measure your workout intensity.

Walking is easy, it's safe and it's inexpensive. You can fit it into even the busiest daily schedule, and not only can you do it alone, you can do it with your spouse, your partner, your children, your friends, your work colleagues, even your grand-parents. Walking is the oldest form of exercise known to man and has always been his main means of transport. But it's only in the past few decades, as more and more people have become sedentary and inactive, that the physical and mental benefits of walking have become apparent.

WALKING'S HEALTH BENEFITS

'Walking is structurally an almost automatic hydrodynamic process, more beautiful and efficient than man's most advanced machine.'

FRED A. STUTMAN, MD

If you have never felt the rhythm of a good walk in your own muscles, and the psycho-physical tonic of a brisk walkout in your own mind and body, you don't know what you've been missing. Because of the structure, shape and flexibility of the spine, the human body is better suited to walking than any other aerobic activity. Your body is built for action and movement and, as a means of getting from one place to another, it reaches its highest state of physical perfection in the act of walking. The following are just some of the benefits which walking can give you.

Walking strengthens the heart and lungs

Provided you don't stroll, but pace briskly, walking expands your lung capacity, and the efficiency of your exercising muscles and blood circulation is increased so that muscles and blood can process more oxygen – the aerobic effect. The beneficial effects are borne out by several studies which all found that the least active people are twice as likely to experience heart disease as the most active. More than 40 scientific studies worldwide have shown that moderate physical activity like fitness walking develops cardiovascular health and protects against heart disease. The Paffenburger study in the United States found that walking 2 miles a day can lower your chance of a heart attack by up to 30 per cent.

Walking reduces blood pressure

Scientists have known for years that both exercise and weight loss, independent of each other, can lower blood pressure. Because fitness walking gives the heart an aerobic workout, it helps to make the heart more efficient and at the same time helps the body burn calories, thus reducing body weight.

Walking raises level of 'good' cholesterol

Walking won't reduce high cholesterol – though it helps to eat less saturated fat which you can do by following The Walker's Diet (see Step 3). But fitness walking can alter the ratio of 'good' cholesterol (the so-called HDLs which protect the arteries) to 'bad' cholesterol (the LDLs which clog up the arteries – see pages 199–200 for more details). The more you walk, the more your HDL level will rise.

Walking helps prevent osteoporosis

Walking is a perfect body massage. It improves muscle tone and strength and wards off aching joints and potential bone problems such as osteoporosis – the brittle-bone condition prevalent in the elderly. As a form of weight-bearing activity, walking boosts bone density. As bones gain mass, they grow sturdier and less prone to breaks.

Walking can reduce back pain

More than 90 per cent of people suffer from back pain at some point in their lives. Backs and joints become less flexible as we get older, and this process is exacerbated by an inactive lifestyle and bad posture. Fitness walking helps by working the large muscle groups and strengthening the postural muscles of the legs, buttocks, back and abdomen. 'Taking a walk regularly is one of the best things you can do for your back,' says Dr John Regan of The Texas Back Institute.

WALKING'S WEIGHT-LOSS BENEFITS

Most experts now advise that regular, moderate exercise combined with a healthy low-fat diet is the most efficient way to lose weight and stay healthy and to maintain this balance in the long term. Where diets alone have failed, fitness walking can help you get back to your ideal weight and, combined with The Walker's Diet, help you stay there. Let's consider a few of walking's weight-loss benefits:

Walking burns calories

Lots of them: 180 to 200 every 30 minutes.

Walking depletes fat, not muscle

Dieting without exercising tends to deplete lean body mass – in other words, it burns muscle instead of fat. Walking is a first-class fat-burner.

Walking may raise your metabolic rate

Studies show that you can continue burning calories for several hours after a walk; this is known as the after-burn effect. And regular fitness walking may raise your resting metabolism (the energy our body needs to function at rest), which helps you burn calories more easily.

Walking gives you a sense of control over your body

No longer helpless at the thought of another failed diet, you will feel in charge of your own body. When combined with a healthy diet, walking can burn away those unwanted pounds more quickly and efficiently than diets alone.

WALKING AND WELL-BEING

Walking relieves stress

De-toxify and defuse a stressful lifestyle with regular brisk walks. When the day's tensions build up to screaming point, a brisk aerobic walk will recharge your batteries after tension and stress have drained them of power and energy. And it will help you relax and put you back in control of your life. So instead of reaching for a gin and tonic, take a walking tonic.

Walking lifts mood

Fitness walking lifts your mood in the same way that it helps you to walk away from stress. Calming brain chemicals called endorphins are released into the blood stream during exercise.

These morphine-like chemicals help suppress pain and elevate mood, and physical activity increases their level. Boosting your system with regular brisk walks will lift your spirits and promote feelings of happiness and well-being.

Walking increases energy

Feeling tired and worn out lately? Then rev up your circulation at any time of the day with a brisk ten-minute walk. Fitness walking can prevent large swings in blood-sugar levels, which can dramatically affect mood and energy levels. And the increased uptake of oxygen – the aerobic effect – gives your whole system a boost and makes you feel more alive and vital. So forget the coffee break: take an energy-boosting walk instead.

Whichever way you look at it, walking wins every time.

WHY WE NEED TO EXERCISE

Man has walked upright for several million years, yet it is only since the domestication of the horse about six thousand years ago and the invention of the wheel around five thousand years ago that man has had alternative means of transport. And it was not until the universal building of railways in the mid-nineteenth century that the great mass of the population was able to put its collective feet up. Since then, it has been downhill all the way – from a health and fitness point of view, that is!

'The civilised man has built a coach and lost the use of his feet,' lamented Ralph Waldo Emerson, the American poet, writing in the nineteenth century. The horse, the coach, the railway, the omnibus and finally the motor car have robbed us of our natural birthright. *Homo sapiens* is now *homo sedens* – and that's official. It's not the passing years but a passive lifestyle that's the problem.

'We are under-exercised as a nation. We look instead of play. We ride instead of walk. Our existence deprives us of the minimum of physical activity essential for healthy living.'

JOHN FITZGERALD KENNEDY

And that was the President of the United States talking in the early 1960s. Since then, the situation has gone from bad to worse. In the past 40 years, people following a Western lifestyle have become increasingly inactive – they spend more time on their behinds than on their feet. Physiologists used to say that our bodies declined naturally with the passing years, but it is now accepted wisdom that our bodies decline because we become inactive as we get older. In short, too many of us adopt a couch-potato lifestyle. And it's predicted to get worse.

Labour-saving devices being developed today could leave the human race facing an epidemic of obesity. Technology and robotics experts say that over the next 50 years all physical activities will be replaced or augmented by computers and machinery. Smart kitchens in which cookers, fridge, bin and cupboards interact; house-cleaning robots which can make intelligent decisions; intelligent furniture; home computer networks controlling the interaction of telephones, televisions, video recorders, mobile devices and the Internet – commonplace inventions such as these will all tend to make us more inactive, leaving us more time to sit around watching television. A recent report in *The Times* said that the British spend more than ten years of their waking lives staring at the television.

'Obesity is already a big cause of ill-health and it's going to get worse if people continue to get more inactive as a result of these labour-saving devices,' says Dr Andrew Prentice, a nutrition expert at the London School of Hygiene and Tropical Medicine.

As medical experts called for action to halt the 'epidemic of obesity sweeping the UK', a recent report confirmed that 20 per cent of Britons are now obese (i.e. at least 20 per cent above optimum body weight) and 50 per cent are overweight. And children are not spared. In Britain, the number of officially obese six-year-olds has doubled in the last ten years, while the proportion of obese 15-year-olds has trebled. The situation is no better in the United States, where figures released by the US Center for Disease Control and Prevention at the end of the century showed that 18 per cent of Americans were obese (defined as being 30 per cent above optimum body weight).

Research shows that while poor diet plays its part, inactivity is the chief culprit. As children and adults, we take too little exercise and we spend too much time hunched over computers, slumped in front of the television, or ferrying ourselves and our families around by car. As a result, we are not burning off as many calories as we used to. And unless this situation is reversed and we all make the decision to lead more active lives, there could be epidemics of obesity-related conditions such as diabetes, cardiovascular disease and hypertension.

And it doesn't end there. Inactivity is also connected to problems such as stress, depression, osteoporosis and back pain, all conditions which inhibit our health and fitness. In short, we have to begin taking exercise seriously.

THE BENEFITS OF EXERCISE

When we are fit, we have greater reserves of strength and stamina. Increased strength helps us perform tasks such as removing a difficult jar lid or lifting a heavy load. And stamina gives us the get-up-and-go to get through the day at home and at work without becoming tired. Being fit, quite simply, puts us in control of our lives. But to get fit, we need to exercise.

Studies show that regular, vigorous exercise increases the activity of our whole body. And it does this not only for the period we are exercising, but also in the longer term, by increasing our metabolism (the rate of activity in our bodies). As a result, we have more energy, we feel better physically and psychologically, we sleep better, and our body burns more calories, even at rest, so exercise helps us control our weight.

Exercise improves circulation and strengthens the heart, lungs, bones and muscles. Exercise also controls blood sugar, reduces the level of fats in our blood and lowers blood pressure. Taken as a whole, exercise is the best investment we can make for a long, healthy life.

It often seems that exercise programmes are geared up for people in the prime of life. As a result, the high-tech Lycra-clad image of aerobic exercise and physical fitness puts many people off; they think that fitness is mainly for athletes, sports enthusiasts and the young. But current research shows that fitness is important to all of us, through all stages of life, and especially as we grow older.

We are born bursting with life, our bodies filled with energy, but as we grow older and start to lead more sedentary, inactive lives, this energy is blocked within us. Exercise is the magic bullet which releases the flow of natural energy that is dormant within us. And the good news is that it's never too late to begin. By staying active and exercising regularly, we can maintain stamina and suppleness, as well as our aerobic capacity, even into the last decades of our life. To get fit, we need to exercise, and one of the easiest ways to do this is to walk more often.

THE NEED FOR AEROBIC FITNESS

Any type of exercise is better than none, but the best kind of exercise is regular, vigorous aerobic exercise. Since the 1960s, the benefits of aerobic exercise have been widely researched and medical authorities now recommend that for healthy adults looking to improve their fitness level, aerobic exercise should be performed for 20–30 minutes, five or six days a week. And for complete fitness, including strength and suppleness, the recommendations are that people supplement their aerobic training with strength training and a routine stretching all their major muscle groups two to three times each week.

Aerobic fitness (or cardiovascular fitness) is your body's ability to perform sustained physical activity that taxes your heart above its resting rate. This is important because as you become fit, your heart pumps blood faster and harder in order to supply your working muscles with nutrients and oxygen. Over time, your heart grows stronger and blood flow to the muscles is improved. Since you have to breathe harder, deeper and faster, your lung capacity and efficiency increase, so less effort is expended to process the oxygen your body needs. It's because of this beneficial effect on your health that aerobic fitness is considered the most important component of physical fitness.

Aerobic exercise consists of continuous rhythmic movement using the large muscle groups of the body: exercises such as cycling, swimming, jogging, rowing and cross-country skiing. But one exercise that people do not always associate with aerobic fitness is walking.

Walking is the easiest and safest exercise to build into a lifelong habit. And when it has become a regular habit, a day will not go by without feeling the need to get outside and experience the rhythm of a good walk. It only remains now to make a start by taking a step in the right direction. How? You put your right foot forward. It's that simple.

TAKE A STEP IN THE RIGHT DIRECTION

'The longest journey begins with just one step.'
CHINESE SAYING

Surveys show that 25 per cent of people who start an exercise programme quit in the first week. We've all seen the first-time joggers puffing and panting their way along the pavement as though their lives depended on it. Before long, they've pulled a muscle or injured their knee, and they're out of action for a few weeks. Inevitably, many give up before they've even started.

'Jogging may do wonders for your heart,' says Sarah Key, physiotherapist to the Prince of Wales. 'But it'll do little for your joints.'

Yet it doesn't have to be like that. You don't have to strain yourself with 'no pain, no gain' exercises which can do more harm than good. Walking is the easiest way to exercise to an aerobic level, simply because we all walk anyway, and have been doing so since we were toddlers. It's just that in the meantime many of us have adopted a more passive lifestyle and are consequently unfit and out of condition. So, if we are to avoid the injury–quit syndrome, we need to make sure that we begin slowly, at a level we find comfortable and can gradually improve on.

You can assess your level of fitness using the following three-step plan. If your lifestyle has been passive for some time and you are completely unfit, then beginning with Level 1 will ease you into a regular walking routine. If you are moderately fit and exercise a little already, then you might prefer to begin with Level 2. If, on the other hand, you are fit and do regular aerobic exercise, then you can go straight to Level 3 in the next chapter and begin your 30-Day Walking Workout.

Level 1

Completely unfit; mainly sedentary occupation and lifestyle; no regular exercise for several years; would get out of breath walking up a gentle gradient or running for a bus.

Level 2

Moderately fit, such as a casual walker, cyclist or swimmer; lifestyle involving standing or movement; not used to exercising at an aerobic level demanding vigorous exertion several times a week.

Level 3

Fit, energetic and focused; lifestyle and job requires a lot of movement and activity; exercising regularly – three to four times a week using aerobic exercise such as fitness walking, jogging, cycling or swimming.

LEVEL 1: STEP TO THE RHYTHM – THE 7-DAY WALKOUT PLAN

Whether you're young or old, walking is an easy and safe way to get fit and stay fit. But it's still important to start slowly. Level 1 gets you started and gradually builds up to a regular, habit-forming walking routine over seven days. At this level, the only thing that matters is the time you put in, not distance or speed. So let's step it out.

Your goal should be a ten-minute walk. Simply step out of your own front door and walk for five minutes along a familiar route at your normal walking pace. Then turn around and come home. It's that simple. As you walk, it's a good idea to bear in mind one or two posture pointers to help you stay focused and ensure your body alignment is correct. Keep your head level, your chin parallel to the ground, your eyes looking straight ahead (not down), and relax your shoulders, keeping them back and down.

How fast should I walk?

During your ten-minute walk, you will have been using the large muscle groups in your legs and arms and you will have elevated your heart rate sufficiently to give you an increased feeling of vitality and well-being. And you will be creating a habit that you will be able to keep up for the rest of your life. But just one word of caution: even though walking is a low-intensity, moderate exercise, it is still possible to overdo it, particularly if you are unfit and have been inactive for some time. So take it gently and listen to your body. You may be slightly breathless, but you shouldn't be out of breath. If you are, then slow down to a more comfortable pace. And note whether you feel any specific aches or pains. If you do, then ease off, and take a day's rest from walking if necessary. If you walk within your own fitness ability at all times, your walks should be injury-free and you will have the desire and motivation to make further progress.

Add variety to your walks

On Day 2, you can either clock up another ten-minute walkout around your planned route or you can add some variety to your walks to make them more interesting. You could build a walk into your journey to work, get off the bus early, or park further away from the office. Or you could save the expense of driving to the shops and walk instead. Or involve the family, a friend or a work colleague. Another variation is to walk at different times of the day: morning, afternoon, or evening. There are so many ways you can fit a ten-minute walk into your daily routine.

A good idea is to plan for a rest day on Day 4 or 5, especially if you began the week out of condition. If, after three or four days, you can manage a ten-minute walk without getting out of breath or tired, then you can move straight on to the 7-Day Walkfit Plan. But if you feel more comfortable sticking with ten-minute walks, then continue with them for another week, maybe longer, making sure that you take a rest day every four or five days, until you feel ready to begin the 7-Day Walkfit Plan.

LEVEL 2: PUT YOUR HEART INTO IT – THE 7-DAY WALKFIT PLAN

If you are starting at Level 2, first take a few minutes to read through the walking tips in Level 1.

Level 2 is designed to ease you gently into brisk aerobic walking and to prepare you for the increasing amounts of exertion required by the 30-Day Walking Workout. Working out at Level 2 assumes you can walk at a moderate pace for ten minutes without getting tired or out of breath. So that's where it begins – but on Days 1 and 2 you begin to increase your time gradually from ten to 15 minutes.

Then, on Days 3 and 4, you begin walking a little faster and step up to a brisk pace. What's a brisk pace? To begin with, a speed that demands a little more exertion than your normal walking pace – for example, walking quickly to catch a bus. A good gauge is to step out with a partner or friend at a faster-than-normal pace but still be able to hold a conversation without getting out of breath. If you feel breathless, then slow down to a comfortable pace. As you get fitter, you'll be able to walk faster without getting out of breath.

After a rest day, continue at a brisk pace so that by Day 7 you'll be able to take a 20-minute walk in your stride. At this point, you can either repeat the 7-Day Walkfit Plan, or, if you feel ready, move on to the 30-Day Walking Workout.

The 7-Day Walkfit Plan

	pace	time planned
Day 1	Moderate	10–15
Day 2	Moderate	10–15
Day 3	Moderate to brisk	15
Day 4	Moderate to brisk	15–20
Day 5	–	Rest
Day 6	Brisk	15–20
Day 7	Brisk	20

STEP
TWO

The 30-Day Walking Workout

'I have sometimes thought it would be well to publish
an Art of Walking, with Easy Lessons for Beginners.'
                                                RALPH WALDO EMERSON

None of us knows what the next 30 days may hold for us, but
the one thing we do know is that 30 days can make a difference.
In 30 days the moon changes from a tiny sickle to a full moon
then shrinks back to a crescent again. And 30 days is enough
time to start fitness walking and to build a healthy eating routine
that will last you a lifetime.

The 30-Day Walking Workout is a comprehensive guide to
the changes you need to make in your life if you are to
become healthier and fitter, and which will get you back in
shape and bounding with energy. This is your 30-day plan.
You are in control. It's now up to you to step out each day and
make the changes that will lead to a fitter, slimmer, more
active you.

The key to starting and staying with an exercise and healthy-
eating programme is motivation. Motivation is the stimulant
that gets you going and keeps you going through the ups and
downs that are inevitable when you set out to make changes in
your life. And the greatest motivator is knowing that what you
are doing works and works quickly.

You have your mind set on success, and that's crucial,
because over the coming 30 days you will need to believe in
your own ability to make the effort necessary to succeed. But
having a 'game plan', tailored to your own lifestyle, is the best
route to success. Here are a few ways to help you achieve your
target.

1   Seek support

You may find it easier to keep up a regular routine if you involve a friend, a member of the family or a work colleague. If you can't find anyone in your immediate circle, put up a notice on the bulletin board at work or in your local fitness centre. Or you could consider starting your own walking club, perhaps during a lunch hour or after work.

2   Schedule your workouts

The best way to build a regular habit is to walk at the same time each day. But first, it's a good idea to experiment with different times until you find your personal 'best time'. It may be morning, lunchtime, or early evening. Whatever time it is, make a mental note (or a written one in your diary) to schedule your walk each day at the same time.

3   Invest in success

Gear yourself up for success by treating yourself to a new pair of walking shoes. A supportive and comfortable shoe is the main piece of equipment you need, and having the right kit will increase your confidence and put some zip into your step. For some tips on how to buy a good 'walkable' shoe, take a look at pages 163–64.

4   Keep track

A good motivational aid is to start a walking log. It doesn't need to be anything fancy – just a few simple headings such as day, pace, time planned (minutes), time walked (minutes), route taken, comments and feelings (about surroundings, weather, and so on). You may want to add a few more headings such as speed and distance, and a column for weekly totals. By keeping track and recording your walks, you will create a kind of ongoing feedback which you can use to chart your progress.

PLANNING YOUR WALKING WORKOUTS

When you begin your 30-Day Walking Workout, you will either be starting out at Level 3, or you will have completed the 7-Day Walkfit routine. Either way, you will be able to walk for 20 minutes without getting tired or breathless. But before you step up the pace in the 30-Day Plan, you need to give some thought to warming up and cooling down.

If you take a look at the layout of the 30-Day Plan on page 34, you will see that after the total number of minutes suggested to walk each day, there are three main headings: warm-up, target zone and cool-down. If you skim through the days quickly, you will note that each walk begins with a five-minute warm-up, followed by the target-zone pace and time for the day, and ends with a five-minute cool-down. Although walking is a safe, low-impact exercise using muscles that you have been using all your life, warming up and cooling down will help you improve your performance and prevent injuries.

HOW TO WARM UP

The best way to warm up is to walk slowly (your normal walking pace) for five minutes before stepping up to the target-zone brisk pace required each day. The body is like a finely tuned machine that needs to be warmed up if it is to work at maximum efficiency. A warm-up prepares the body for exercise by gradually increasing your heart rate, breathing rate and blood circulation. As your body temperature rises, your muscles warm up and joints are lubricated in readiness for action, reducing the risk of injury. Increasing the blood supply to muscles provides them with more oxygen and glucose, enabling you to establish a strong aerobic pace early in your workout. Warming up also increases blood flow to the brain which improves your mood, focus and motivation.

How to cool down

The best way to cool down is to gently reduce your pace over five minutes from the target-zone pace to your normal walking pace, so that your heart rate and blood pressure can begin to return to normal. A cool-down after aerobic walking is as important as a warm-up beforehand. A proper cool-down keeps the blood flowing through the muscles and any lactic acid that has built up inside the muscle cells can be dispersed in the circulation to the liver, where it is broken down. By doing this you should avoid niggling problems such as cramps, muscle soreness and stiffness.

Post-walk stretches

Although warm-ups before a walk and cool-downs afterwards are important, after exercising at a brisk pace you should also wind down with a few muscle-stretching and -loosening exercises to prevent soreness and injury. At the end of your walk, the muscles are warm and this is therefore the perfect time to stretch safely and effectively.

The first four stretches exercise the main muscle groups you use when you walk: the quadriceps (the large muscle group on the front of the thigh), the hamstrings (the back of the thigh), and the calves and Achilles tendons found at the back of the lower leg from the knee down towards the heel.

As you perform the stretches, aim to progress gradually without straining yourself. The number of repetitions and the length of time given here are only a guide; you can reduce or increase them to suit yourself. Always ease into your stretches, using smooth, slow movements. If you feel any strain, then ease off, go on to another exercise, or leave that particular exercise out until you are ready to try again another day. If you listen to your own body, you won't go far wrong.

1   Calf stretch

Bend left knee, keeping it directly over left heel, and extend right leg back, with right heel flat to the floor and toes pointing straight ahead. With a straight back, ease chest forward, supporting upper body weight with hands on left thigh. Keep abdominals pulled in and head up. Feel the stretch down the back of the calf as the heel is pressed to the floor. Hold for 15–20 seconds. Repeat with other leg.

2   Hamstring stretch

Bend right leg, placing hands on right thigh to support upper body weight. Stretch left leg out in front of you, toes pointed and knee slightly bent. Keep your head up and abdominals in as you lean forward slightly from the hip. Keep your back straight as the tailbone is gently pushed back. Feel stretch behind left thigh. Hold for 15–20 seconds. Remember that stretches should always feel comfortable (a mild tension). Repeat with other leg.

To increase this stretch, especially after walking or other exercise, gently lift toes on extended leg and hold.

3   Quadriceps stretch

Stand tall with knees slightly bent (using a wall or any solid object for balance if necessary). Hold on to left ankle and lift the left foot up and back towards the left buttock. Keep the knees together and tuck the bottom under. Hold for 10–20 seconds. Lower the foot to the floor and repeat on the other side.

4 Lower calf and Achilles tendon stretch

5 Lower back stretch

Place hands on wall at shoulder height. Keep feet together, with toes forward and heels down, about 2 feet from wall. Keeping bottom tucked under, slowly bend knees until stretch is felt in lower calves and Achilles tendons. Hold for 10 seconds.

Stand with feet just wider than hip-width apart, with knees bent and hands on thighs supporting weight of upper body. Tuck bottom under and round the back, pulling in abdominals. Hold for 6 counts. Release and repeat 3 times.

6   Upper back stretch   7   Chest stretch

Stand with feet hip-width apart, knees slightly bent, bottom tucked under and abdominals pulled in. Stretch out arms in front of you, clasping hands together. Relax chin to chest and round and separate shoulders to feel stretch across upper back. Hold for 6 counts. Release and repeat.

Stand as before, looking forward. Relax shoulders down and clasp hands together behind back. Slowly extend arms as you lift them up behind back. Hold for 4 counts. Release and repeat.

8   Shoulder stretch

Stand as before, with abdominals in and bottom tucked under. Place one hand between shoulder and elbow. Gently press arm towards opposite shoulder. Hold for 6 counts. Repeat with other arm.

Your 30-Day Walking Workout at a Glance

day	warm-up	target zone	cool-down	total
	walk slowly	walk briskly	walk slowly	
1	5	10	5	20
2	5	10	5	20
3	5	10	5	20
4	5	10	5	20
5	–	rest day	–	0
6	5	10	5	20
7	5	10–15	5	20–25
8	5	10–15	5	20–25
9	5	10–15	5	20–25
10	5	15	5	25
11	–	rest day	–	0
12	5	15	5	25
13	5	15–20	5	25–30
14	5	15–20	5	25–30
15	5	15–20	5	25–30

Your 30-Day Walking Workout at a Glance (*continued*)

day	warm-up	target zone	cool-down	total
	walk slowly	walk briskly	walk slowly	
16	5	20	5	30
17	–	rest day	–	0
18	5	20	5	30
19	5	20	5	30
20	5	20–25	5	30–35
21	5	20–25	5	30–35
22	5	20–25	5	30–35
23	5	25	5	35
24	–	rest day	–	0
25	5	25	5	35
26	5	25–30	5	35–40
27	5	25–30	5	35–40
28	5	25–30	5	35–40
29	5	30	5	40
30	5	30	5	40

DAY 1
20 minutes

warm-up	target zone	cool-down
walk slowly	*walk briskly*	*walk slowly*
5	10	5

One step forward

It's important on Day 1 to visualise not only the day ahead, but also the remaining days in your 30-Day Workout. By keeping your mind firmly on your goal, you will find it much easier to get motivated and stay motivated. So let's step it out.

Day 1 can be any day you choose, but Monday seems like a good day to take the first steps towards a new, fitter, more energetic you. Simply head out of the door and walk for 20 minutes around the route you have planned, remembering first to warm up. Warm up by gradually increasing your pace over five minutes, allowing your heart rate to rise into its aerobic zone.

How fast should you walk?

Try taking the fitness-walk test. If you can't hold a conversation while you walk, you are going too fast. By stepping out with the longest stride that is comfortable, you will gradually build up to a steady rhythm. It can take five to ten minutes to get into a good rhythm and get the circulation going, but once you get going, you will find it easy to keep going. If at any time you feel yourself straining, reduce your pace until you feel comfortable again. A good tip is to learn to listen to your own body – it's always right.

As you come to the end of your walk, cool down by gradually decreasing your pace over five minutes until you finish.

That wasn't too difficult, was it? Finish the day by sitting calmly and visualising Day 30 – the final day, when you will be a fully-fledged fitness walker.

Footnotes
'One of the pleasantest things in the world is going on a journey.'   WILLIAM HAZLITT

DAY 2
20 minutes

warm-up	target zone	cool-down
walk slowly	*walk briskly*	*walk slowly*
5	10	5

Kick-start your morning

Many of us start the day half-awake, dragging our listless bodies around all morning until they are warmed up around lunchtime, when we feel ready for the rest of the day. What we really need is a morning energiser to kick-start our metabolism and get us going.

There are good reasons why we feel sluggish as the day begins. Somewhere around 3 a.m. to 5 a.m. each morning, our hormone levels are depressed and our heart rate and body temperature are lower than normal. So when the alarm goes off and all we want to do is turn over and go back to sleep, we really do feel like death warmed up. But instead of always giving in to that lethargic, 'Do I really have to get up?' feeling, why not try a 15–20 minute aerobic walk? An early-morning walkout gets you going, warms up your body and your mind, and gives you a physical and psychological edge on the day. First thing in the morning, an early-morning energy-boosting walk will do you far more good than an extra 15 minutes in bed, and it's far healthier than a cup of coffee.

Caution: Generally speaking, a five-minute slow walk should be enough for your body to warm up. But on cold mornings, or mornings when you feel a bit of extra stiffness in the joints, you might want to warm up before leaving the house. Use a few of the warm-ups in the Bodywise section (see pages 126–31).

Morning meditation

Your early-morning walk can be a special time of the day: your own calm space in which to plan the day ahead. Being mentally and physically prepared will give you the focus, energy and stamina to cope with the day.

Footnotes
'An early morning walk is a blessing for the whole day.'

HENRY DAVID THOREAU

DAY 3
20 minutes

warm-up	target zone	cool-down
walk slowly	walk briskly	walk slowly
5	10	5

Walk this way

The key to effortless walking is good posture and an effective walking rhythm. So today we're going to focus on five techniques that will help you zip along at an easy, comfortable pace.

Walk tall. Concentrate on lengthening your body from your toes to the top of your head. To help you do this, try imagining a piece of string running up through your body and out of the top of your head, reaching towards the sky. Then imagine you're a puppet being pulled upwards by the string.

Head up. The way you hold your head can affect your entire posture. Just watch the way some people hold their heads when they're walking: with their heads down and chins tucked in, their bodies are out of natural alignment. If you walk with your head level, chin parallel to the ground and eyes focused straight ahead, you will feel better both mentally and physically. To supply your muscles with oxygen, inhale and exhale rhythmically.

Shoulders back and down. As you walk, keep your back straight, with the weight of your body slightly in front of your ankles. Now relax your shoulders: keep them back and down, opening up the chest, and keep your elbows close to the sides of your body.

Abdominal muscles pulled in. Pull in your stomach and flatten the small of your back by tucking in your buttocks under your spine – this technique is known as the 'pelvic tilt'. This will provide support for your lower back and will help you maintain your most comfortable walking posture.

Walk at an easy, comfortable pace. To develop a natural rhythm, take the longest stride that is comfortable, not placing your feet too far apart, and lead with your hips, letting your arms swing naturally in opposition to your legs.

Footnotes

At the end of the day, pamper your feet with a long soak in the bath. Add a dash of aromatherapy oil, or splash out and buy yourself a foot spa. If you look after your feet, you'll enjoy endless miles of troublefree walking.

DAY 4
20 minutes

warm-up	target zone	cool-down
walk slowly	*walk briskly*	*walk slowly*
5	10	5

Weighty issues

Walking might not be the quickest way to lose weight, but it is
the easiest and safest way, and the results usually last for longer.
Just look at the facts: a 150-pound person walking briskly at
3½–4 miles per hour will burn off on average 180–200 calories
every 30 minutes. A 200-pound person walking at the same
speed will burn around 235–265 calories every 30 minutes. To
simplify matters, let's say that the average person can lose
around 100 calories for every 15 minutes of brisk walking. Now,
if you add up all the ways during the week that you can fit in a
15-minute brisk walk, it equals an awful lot of calories every
week. Bear in mind that your body burns fat more efficiently
when you walk briskly for at least 30 minutes.

Of course, walking burns calories at any speed, and brisk walking burns more. But if you are unable to walk fast, or you don't
want to, then simply spend more time on your walks to make up
the difference. You really can't lose! And by combining your
aerobic walks with the nutritional advice in the 30-Day Healthy-
Eating Plan, you can lose weight effortlessly in a more pleasurable
way than with any traditional diet or weight-loss scheme.

Powering up your cells

Your body is made up of millions of minute living units called
cells. These cells make up your blood, bones, skin, muscles,

nerves and all the other parts of your body. Within cells are tiny structures called mitochondria, and these act like fat-guzzling engines that help burn up calories. And as regular walking increases the size and number of mitochondria, the more you walk, the more mitochondria you have in your cells, and the more fat you burn. And research has shown that you will continue to burn calories long after your walk is over. So don't delay – hit the road today!

Footnotes

'Walking is crucial to every diet plan.'

DR JAMES RIPPE AND ANN WARD, EXERCISE PHYSIOLOGY AND NUTRITIONAL LABORATORY, UNIVERSITY OF MASSACHUSETTS

DAY 5
0 minutes

rest day

Practise the foot roll

In order to generate more speed, as you step out, push off with the ball and toes of your back foot and land in the middle of your front heel. Avoid slapping the toes down, since this can cause shin soreness. Then roll forward through the instep and ball of the foot and push off the toes to take your next step. If you practise this technique, you'll develop a smooth, rhythmic flow to your walking action.

Now try putting all the techniques you have learned together: walking tall, with your head level, shoulders back and down, abdominals pulled in, rolling your feet from heel to toe. The diagram overleaf will help to make you more mindful of the way you hold your body when you walk.

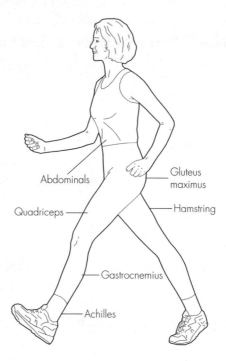

Abdominals

Gluteus maximus

Quadriceps

Hamstring

Gastrocnemius

Achilles

Footnotes

'The mental pleasure in walking is in the sense of power over all our moving machinery.'
OLIVER WENDELL HOLMES

DAY 6
20 minutes

warm-up	target zone	cool-down
walk slowly	*walk briskly*	*walk slowly*
5	10	5

Fit fitness into your day

To keep your interest and motivation going, you need to discover new ways to make walking part of your life, so we are now going to show you six creative ways to get the most out of your walks and keep them varied and, above all, fun.

Change your normal routine. By getting off the bus or train one or two stops early or leaving your car a distance from your destination and walking the rest of the way, you can add variety to your walks – and lose a few hundred calories along the way.

Walk during a lunch break. Make a point of getting out of the home or office at lunchtime, even if it's for only a short break. It will re-energise you and break up the day's routine. To make your walks interesting and to help keep you motivated, invite a friend or colleague, or start a lunchtime walking group.

Climb stairs each day. Instead of taking the easy option, let others use the lift while you climb the stairs. It will make your heart beat faster and will help build stamina to get you through the day.

Add a detour to a journey. To clock up extra energy-boosting miles, schedule a detour into a journey. Or simply take the scenic route to your destination.

Walk in the evening. A brisk walk before a meal, or a slow stroll after a meal, will work off weight and help you relax and de-stress.

Organise weekend walks. Planning a weekend jaunt to the countryside, the seaside, or a special place of interest will give you something to look forward to during the week and will break your normal routine.

Footnotes

Walking is an excellent foundation exercise for other aerobic activities such as swimming, cycling and low-impact aerobics.

DAY 7
20–25 minutes

warm-up	target zone	cool-down
walk slowly	*walk briskly*	*walk slowly*
5	10–15	5

Workout with water

One half to three-quarters of the body's weight is water. You can live for weeks without food, but only a few days without water. Water is the body's single most essential nutrient and is as necessary to a healthy lifestyle as exercise and a nutritious diet. Required by all the body's biological functions, water regulates, among other things, body temperature and blood volume, and it lubricates your joints.

Don't wait until you're thirsty before drinking water. The body is constantly losing water through perspiration, breathing and in the elimination of body wastes, so to compensate for this dehydration, you need to drink water before, during and after exercise. Recommended consumption is about six to eight glasses a day.

Although other drinks may contribute to your fluid intake each day, drinks containing caffeine or alcohol actually dehydrate the body, so you lose fluid. It's safer to stick with your water workout.

Mind–body focus

Many people start exercising but then fail, because the exercises are too difficult, or they get injured. The beauty of walking is that you can gradually increase the intensity of your workout without the fear of failure or injury. Because walking works, it is easier to keep motivated and focused on making the sort of health and fitness gains that really add up.

So, on Day 7, as you come to the end of your first week, consider the progress you have made, and empower yourself with positive thoughts. Use a few simple affirmations to reinforce your gains: 'I am organised and in control of my life. I have the motivation to get out there every day and keep going. I have my 30-day goal in sight.' Now focus on your objectives for the following week by previewing Days 8–14. Then visualise yourself confidently striding out each day to meet your goal.

Footnotes
'Water is outstanding in doing good.'

LAO-TSE

DAY 8
20–25 minutes

warm-up	target zone	cool-down
walk slowly	*walk briskly*	*walk slowly*
5	10–15	5

Stepping up the pace

As you step up your pace, you're really beginning to turn your walks into workouts. So you probably want to know how fast you're walking. A rough rule of thumb is to count how many steps you take each minute. The following table calculates your speed based on three common stride lengths. To measure your stride length, walk ten steps forward. Measure the distance covered, then divide the distance by ten to arrive at your stride length.

Steps per minute			Minutes	Miles
2-foot stride	$2\frac{1}{2}$-foot stride	3-foot stride	per mile	per hour
90	70	60	30	2
110	90	75	24	$2\frac{1}{2}$
130	105	90	20	3
155	120	105	17	$3\frac{1}{2}$
175	140	120	15	4
200	160	135	13	$4\frac{1}{2}$
220	175	145	12	5

Measure out an exact mile

An alternative to counting your steps is to take a car ride around the route you intend to use for your regular walk, and use the car's odometer to measure the distance between two familiar landmarks. If you know exactly how long a mile is, then all you have to do is time yourself during the mile walk. If it takes you 15 minutes to walk a mile, you are walking at 4 miles per hour, calculated as:

$$\text{Speed} \ = \ \frac{\text{Distance}}{\text{Time}} \ = \ \frac{1 \text{ mile}}{0.25 \text{ hours}}$$

If you move away from familiar routes and landmarks, you might want to acquire a gadget called a pedometer. If you clip this on to your belt and adjust it to your stride length, it will calculate the distance you have walked.

Footnotes
Try using a pedometer: an inexpensive gadget that measures your walking distance.

DAY 9
20–25 minutes

warm-up	target zone	cool-down
walk slowly	*walk briskly*	*walk slowly*
5	10–15	5

Smell the breeze

It's said that the difference between a good walker and a bad one is that one walks with his heart and the other with his feet. When seasoned travellers evoke their feelings about 'the spirit of place', they often refer to 'smelling the breeze'. To smell the breeze is to feel one's presence in the moment, body and soul – in the 'now' of one's experience; to move beyond the endless chatter going on in one's head, into a more timeless, tranquil state of mind. Yet it's more than simply a sense of smell. It's a fusion of all one's senses finely tuned to the reality of the moment. Almost a Zen experience – an epiphany.

So why are we telling you this? Because walking can be much more than just a fitness and weight-loss workout. It can be a chance to find a calm space in your day and spend some quality time with yourself. We like to call it 'inner walking' – a way to connect with the deeper reality of our lives. For a change today, step into a comfortable rhythm, then let the distractions within your mind melt away and sample the meditative benefits of inner walking.

Mind–body focus

We spend so much of our day indoors and inside our own heads that we need to get outside in the open air to get back in touch with reality and the natural world around us. We need to wake up and smell the breeze. Outside in the open air, away from the restrictions of the workaday world and workaday cares and pressures, our senses become sharper and more focused and we can see things whole. Outside, we can find the space just to be ourselves. To sample inner walking, you may need a device to dissolve the 'inner chatter', so try repeating the phrase: 'Relax . . . and release . . . Relax . . . and release . . . Relax . . . and release.'

Footnotes

'All walking is discovery. On foot we take the time to see things whole.'

HAL BORLAND

DAY 10
25 minutes

warm-up	target zone	cool-down
walk slowly	*walk briskly*	*walk slowly*
5	15	5

How to measure the intensity of your workout

What is a brisk workout? How hard should you be working out? One of the easiest ways to gauge how hard you are working out is to monitor how you feel. The Borg scale below is based on your sense, or gut feeling, of how hard you are exercising. As you stride out and begin to walk faster, you should aim for Level 4, an intensity which you feel is 'somewhat hard'. This should give you a good aerobic workout.

Borg's Scale of Perceived Exertion

0	No Exertion
1	Very Light
2	Fairly Light
3	
4	Somewhat Hard
5	
6	Hard
7	
8	Very Hard
9	
10	Very, Very Hard

(Based on Borg Rate of Perceived Exertion Scale, © Gunnar Borg, *Medicine and Science in Sports and Exercise*, 1982.)

You will recognise what feels 'somewhat hard'. After you have passed through the 'light' phase during your five-minute warm-up and you hit your target-zone pace, you should feel as if you are pushing hard, but not too hard, as if your walk is giving you a real workout. Remember the other two guides to help you gauge how hard you are working out? If you are getting out of breath, or you are unable to hold a conversation, you are walking too fast. Experiment at different levels of intensity until you find your own comfortable workout pace.

Footnotes
'Work apace, apace, apace, apace;
Honest labour bears a lovely face'
                                                    THOMAS DEKKER

DAY 11
0 minutes

rest day

Take 15-minute walking breaks

Whether at work or at home, forego the caffeine fix and take short walking breaks instead. By adding as little as one 15-minute walking break to your day, you could burn up to 35,000 calories in a year (depending on body weight, a 15-minute brisk walk will burn 80–100 calories). Since each pound of stored body fat equates to 3500 calories, that means that you will burn up to 10 pounds of excess fat a year. By junking that chocolate bar or slice of cake, you can shave another 300 calories from your diet each day. Imagine all those extra calories you could burn in a year by following this simple routine. And you will become fitter, healthier and slimmer in the process. Little changes really can make a big difference!

Mind–body focus

Several times a week, step aside from your normal routine and practise walking meditation. Remember the mantra: 'Relax . . . and release . . . Relax . . . and release . . . Relax . . . and release.'

As you begin to experience the calming effect of walking meditation, and empty your mind of the day's distractions, you may find you naturally become more creative and intuitive. It seems like a paradox, but when you empty your mind of 'inner chatter', ideas and solutions to problems often just pop into your mind, as if by magic. At this point, it's a good idea to start an 'inner walking' diary. After your walk, spend a few minutes jotting down all those key moments – any sights, sounds, sensations and thoughts that came to you during your walk. The trick is to write quickly without too much thought or editing. Just pour out your soul on to the paper, or maybe on your computer. Days or even weeks later, when you return to look over your jottings, you will surprise yourself. Patterns will begin to emerge which can provide a real insight into who you really are. Why not make a poem or a collage out of them?

Footnotes

'Every path, every street in the world is your walking meditation path.'

THICH NHAT HANH

DAY 12
25 minutes

warm-up	target zone	cool-down
walk slowly	walk briskly	walk slowly
5	15	5

Put your heart into it

In Britain today, half the population is overweight, and that goes for the young, too. The number of officially obese six-year-olds has doubled in the last ten years, while the proportion of obese 15-year-olds has trebled. Obesity is the cause of known health risks as we get older, particularly an increased chance of heart disease, high blood pressure and diabetes. While poor diet plays a part, inactivity is the main culprit. Studies show that inactivity can be as bad for us as smoking 20 cigarettes a day, having high levels of blood cholesterol or high blood pressure. A sedentary lifestyle robs people of their fitness and their right to a healthy life, and it places untold demands on the National Health Service.

The message is simple: we all need to ensure that we keep active. And what is the easiest and safest way for most people to get back on their feet again and become more active? Walking. 'Walking offers significant health benefits, especially for the heart. Just 30 minutes of brisk walking, five times a week, is enough to help reduce the risk of coronary heart disease,' says Dr Vivienne Press, assistant medical director at the British Heart Foundation. 'Walking can be easily included into one's daily routine.'

Dozens of scientific studies worldwide have shown that brisk walking develops cardiovascular health and protects against heart disease. The famous Paffenburger study in the United States found that walking 2 miles a day can lower your chance of a heart attack by up to 30 per cent. So to keep your heart in good shape, over the next few days gradually increase your walks to 30 minutes, knowing that you can look forward to a longer, fitter and healthier life.

Footnotes

'I have two doctors, my left leg and my right.'

G. M. Trevelyan

DAY 13
25–30 minutes

warm-up	target zone	cool-down
walk slowly	*walk briskly*	*walk slowly*
5	15–20	5

Walking on air

Brisk walking gives you an aerobic workout, which is important for your heart, your general fitness, and your waistline. Aerobic means 'with oxygen', and walking aerobically powers the body to process more oxygen with less effort. Since oxygen cannot be stored, our cells need a continuous supply in order to stay healthy.

The key benefit of aerobic exercise is an improvement in the vital efficiency of the heart and lungs. Blood vessels enlarge and become more elastic and total blood volume can actually increase, making more red blood cells available to carry oxygen and nutrients to the tissues. Blood flow to the muscles is improved; muscles and ligaments are strengthened; and joints become stronger and more mobile. And the capacity of the lungs is enlarged, enabling them to take in more oxygen. Is it any wonder that walking has become today's smart exercise?

Today, get fit quicker by trying some of the following ways to burn more oxygen, more calories and more fat:

- Walk at around 3½ mph for an effective fat-burning speed and a good, aerobic workout. It's a speed you should be able to keep up for a long time without tiring. And it's the fastest way to get fit and stay fit.
- Bend your arms at about a 90-degree angle at the elbows, then swing them forward and back as you walk, keeping your elbows close to your body. Keep your hands closed,

but don't clench them. Your shoulders should remain
relaxed throughout the arm-swing. A high-energy arm-
swing can help you burn up to 20 per cent more calories.
• Find a park or a hilly area. Walking on grass or uneven
ground will give you an increased calorie burn and a further
30–50 per cent increase in energy expenditure.
• Climb a few flights of stairs a day and burn another 15
calories, which translates to a 1½-pound fat loss each year.

Footnotes

Resist using remote controls for the television and video. Make
the effort to stir yourself from the sofa. And avoid sitting still
for long periods. Get up and take a brisk aerobic walk instead.

DAY 14
25–30 minutes

warm-up	target zone	cool-down
walk slowly	walk briskly	walk slowly
5	15–20	5

Walking with the seasons

One of the attractions of walking is that there are few good
excuses not to do it. And that includes the weather. There are
few days in the year when the weather is either so hot or cold
that we can't fit in a walk at some time during the day. Simply
dress for the weather and pick the best time for your walk.
Here are a few suggestions for walking with the seasons.

Hot weather. During hot weather, wear light-coloured clothes
to reflect the heat and light. Although cotton is comfortable,
when you sweat, it gets wet and tends to stay wet. So go for

synthetic fibres, such as polypropylene, that wick moisture away from the skin and dry quickly. If you're walking in the sun, it's a good idea to wear a brimmed hat.

Cold weather. On cold days, the trick is to make sure your extremities are kept warm. Cover your head and neck, and wear gloves. And wear several light layers of clothing that you can add or remove while you walk. Start with an inner layer of synthetic wicking materials (such as the ones used in hot weather). Then follow with an insulating layer, such as wool or a lightweight fleece material, with a zipper to allow you to warm up or cool down during your walk. Your outer layer should be water-resistant and wind-proof.

Never let the rain put you off. Water-resistant fabrics such as Gore-Tex or Sympatex are light, they breathe, and they work. They may not be cheap, but they are a good investment for walking in inclement weather.

Don't forget to do a few quick stretches when you have finished your walk.

Footnotes
'Not snow, no, nor rain, nor heat, nor night keeps them from accomplishing their appointed courses with all speed.'
HERODOTUS (485–425 BC)

DAY 15
25–30 minutes

warm-up	target zone	cool-down
walk slowly	*walk briskly*	*walk slowly*
5	15–20	5

Maintaining momentum and motivation

The cumulative benefits of following the walking and healthy-eating advice in the 30-Day Plan will now be starting to add up. You should have more energy and vitality, and if you are trying to lose weight, you should be losing a minimum of 1 to 2 pounds each week. That's a good, steady way to lose weight and keep it off. Better than the crazy yo-yo dieting approach which leaves you no slimmer and depressed into the bargain. It's maintaining a steady momentum and making gradual changes in your exercise and diet, week in, week out, that produces results – results that will last in the long term. And these results will inspire you and keep you motivated.

As you step up the pace again this week, don't try to dodge the warm-up and cool-down. These few minutes at the beginning and end of your walk will ensure that you stay free of pulled muscles and other injuries. And remember to fill in your walking log. Not only is it a way of congratulating and rewarding yourself, but it builds up a record of achievement over the weeks which you can look back on later. And finally, remember to drink plenty of water to keep your body hydrated.

Mind–body focus

Life is too short to be taken too seriously. So leave your problems behind today and take a more philosophical view of life. Think positive! Give a little thought to your posture – walk tall, head up, shoulders relaxed – and walk with a smile on your face. Look outside of yourself and smile at others you meet along the way. A smile puts you in a positive mood and it may help to do the same for others.

Footnotes

'The soul of a journey is liberty, perfect liberty to think, feel, do just as one pleases.'
                 WILLIAM HAZLITT

DAY 16
30 minutes

warm-up	target zone	cool-down
walk slowly	*walk briskly*	*walk slowly*
5	20	5

Back to basics

'Oh, my aching back!' How many times have we all heard ourselves say that, or listened to someone else's complaint? More than 80 per cent of people in the UK suffer from back pain at some time in their lives, and back pain is the prime cause of absence from work. And over the past thirty years it has been getting worse. During the 1970s, 1980s and 1990s, the incidence of back pain doubled in each decade. Although back pain has many causes, it's no accident that, in the same period, those of us following a Western lifestyle have become increasingly inactive.

A sedentary lifestyle – too much time spent sitting – and poor posture can cause back problems and weaken back muscles. Time spent sitting at the wheel of a car, in front of the television, at a desk, or focused on a computer screen takes its toll on your back. Sitting for long periods of time without stretching shortens certain postural muscles and can cause lower back pain. The problem is compounded because poor posture often results in shallow breathing, which can restrict blood flow to the brain. We are then no longer in control of our own bodies. Is it any wonder that physically and mentally we feel 'stressed', when we put our bodies under such stress? We need to get back to basics.

To begin with, if you sit for long periods during the day, sit up straight, not in a slouched position. Good posture improves breathing and increases blood flow to the brain. And shift your position at least every 20 minutes. Get up, move around, and do a few simple stretches (see pages 26–31). And when you take a break from work, when possible, make it an exercise break instead of a coffee break. A ten-minute aerobic walk will take your mind off work, revitalise you and give you the motivation to get through the rest of the day. But more of that tomorrow.

Footnotes

'Old age comes with the stiffening of the backbone.'

YOGA SAYING

DAY 17
0 minutes

rest day

Treat your back

Yoga teaches that we grow old when our back becomes stiff and we lose suppleness in our back and joints. This affects the roots of the spinal nerves, which can then affect other body functions such as circulation, digestion and respiration. We feel stiff not only physically, but also mentally.

Although back pain can have many causes, lower back pain can often result from our sedentary lifestyles – our years of inactivity. And one of the easiest and safest ways to become active and mobilise the back is to walk. The easing and eradication of lower back pain is one of the most common benefits reported by walkers. Walking affects the spine in positive ways by strengthening muscles in the pelvis and lower back. It provides the exercise required to keep the back and

joints flexible and it's a superb preventive and curative of most
kinds of muscular back pain. However, in order to gain these
benefits you must focus on your posture.

Good posture is critical to walking without pain. Supporting
the weight of the head and upper body puts a stress on the
vertebrae, the cushioning discs between them, and the muscles
and ligaments holding them in place. Any movement that
throws the spine out of its natural alignment, such as leaning
forward, jutting the chin out or hunching the shoulders, is a
prescription for aggravating back pain. The remedy is to be
aware of your posture and walk tall, with your head level,
shoulders relaxed, and abdominals pulled in, taking deep
natural breaths.

It's also important to emphasise that suppleness and
mobility in the back are maintained not only by regular
exercise, such as fitness walking, but also by regular stretching
exercises (see pages 132–42). It's total fitness that strengthens
the back muscles and helps to alleviate aches and pains. So
give your back a treat: walk and stretch regularly.

Footnotes
'Taking a walk regularly is one of the best things you can do
for your back. It promotes muscular development, increases
circulation, and speeds the release of endorphins which
provide a natural "high".' DR JOHN REGAN, TEXAS BACK INSTITUTE

DAY 18
30 minutes

warm-up	target zone	cool-down
walk slowly	*walk briskly*	*walk slowly*
5	20	5

Walking plus

Don't forget: when it comes to weight loss, all calories count, even the non-aerobic ones. Lifestyle activities may not have the same cardiovascular conditioning effect as fitness walking, but they all help to keep your heart healthy. And they all add up at the end of the day.

Gardening tasks such as raking, weeding and trimming burn about 300 calories an hour. And pushing a manual lawnmower can burn between 420 and 480 calories an hour (as many as an hour of tennis). Housework chores such as mopping, scrubbing, and window cleaning without pause can rack up 250 calories an hour, while washing clothes can clock up another 160 calories an hour. For an average game of golf, carrying your own clubs, your body uses 325 calories an hour. These figures are estimates based on a 150-pound person; the actual number of calories burned varies with age, fitness level, calorie intake and metabolic rate.

Walktalk: Can walking help prevent osteoporosis?

The word osteoporosis means 'porous bones'. It affects mainly women over the age of 45, particularly women after the menopause, because of the reduction in the secretion of oestrogen. As women age, the mineral content of their bones decreases and the texture becomes thinner, making them more likely to sustain fractures. But it's never too early for a woman to begin protecting herself against this debilitating disease. The most common form of treatment is the use of calcium-rich foods to increase bone protein and calcium. And physical activity, particularly weight-bearing exercise such as fitness walking, will help prevent age-related bone-density loss. Studies at Tufts University in the United States show that fitness walking for 45 minutes, four days a week, can slow down and halt the development of osteoporosis.

So be your own physician: eat plenty of calcium-rich foods and walk often.

Footnotes

The best sources of calcium are dairy products, particularly milk, yogurt and cheeses (buy the low-fat versions). Non-dairy sources are leafy green vegetables and canned salmon and sardines.

DAY 19
30 minutes

warm-up	target zone	cool-down
walk slowly	*walk briskly*	*walk slowly*
5	20	5

Three quick calorie crushers

If you feel that your stamina has improved and you are able to push yourself a little harder without straining yourself, then try these three ways to burn off those unwanted pounds more quickly.

Walk faster. A 150-pound person burns 300 calories an hour at 3 miles per hour, 370 calories at 3½ miles per hour and 400 calories at 4 miles an hour. But there's a trade-off. Walking faster burns more calories, but it also means there's more chance of injury. If you do decide to walk faster, then don't push too hard. After your warm-up, accelerate gradually into your target-zone speed, walk for the desired time, then reduce speed gradually, ending with a cool-down of slow walking. If at any time you feel sore, then simply ease back to a comfortable speed. Another technique is to try some interval walking. Alternate your normal walking pace with short bursts of faster walking for a few minutes, then repeat a few times.

Remember that intensity isn't everything. A good fat-burning speed for most people is 3½ miles per hour, maintained for at least 30 minutes; it's easy to keep up day in, day out, all the year round. You burn calories by walking longer, rather than harder. The best advice is to experiment and stick with what's comfortable and gets results.

Walk up hills. Hill walking increases your level of cardio-vascular fitness and burns more calories in less time. By walking up a 5 per cent gradient at 4 miles per hour you will burn 50 per cent more calories. On a 10 per cent gradient you will burn 100 per cent more calories.

Walk after meals. A post-meal walk at a moderate pace will help your digestion, increase your energy and burn away some of the calories you have just consumed. And it will help relieve that stuffed, bloated feeling after a meal.

F o o t n o t e s
'Research shows that breaking a daily 30-minute exercise routine into two or three shorter sessions burns 30 per cent more calories after you finish due to the separate after burn.'

UNIVERSITY OF KANSAS

DAY 20
30–35 minutes

warm-up	target zone	cool-down
walk slowly	*walk briskly*	*walk slowly*
5	20–25	5

How to walk safely

With the level of road traffic increasing each year, walkers need to be alert to road safety. Walking together as a family can be an ideal time to focus on this. During family walks you can talk about road safety to your children and impress upon them the need to be aware of their surroundings at all times. The following suggestions will keep you streetwise.

Using the pavement

- Walk on the nearside of the pavement, away from the road edge
- Cross the road at traffic lights or at a recognised crossing point
- Look both ways twice before stepping out into the road and make sure there is time to cross without hurrying
- Watch out for other oncoming pedestrians who may not give way to you, forcing you to step off the pavement onto the road
- Learn to recognise the sounds of other road users – cars, buses, trucks, cyclists and motorcyclists
- At all times follow the basic Highway Code: STOP, LOOK and LISTEN

Using an unpaved road

- Walk facing oncoming traffic, so you can see cars and they can see you
- Day or night, wear bright clothes or fluorescent strips so you can be seen by other road users
- Use your senses: sight, sound and smell – if in doubt stop

© Ray Foan, Accident Risk Reduction Manager, West Berkshire NHS Trust

Footnotes

'Thro' the world we safely go.'   WILLIAM BLAKE

DAY 21
30–35 minutes

warm-up	target zone	cool-down
walk slowly	*walk briskly*	*walk slowly*
5	20–25	5

Moving on: Building long-term habits

Only ten more days to go! By gradually building up your aerobic fitness and following the Healthy-Eating Plan, you should have more energy and vitality and you should be losing some of those unwanted pounds. Don't forget to warm up before and cool down after your walk. And remember to fill in your walking log. As an aid to motivation, it will track your achievement each day and help keep you moving towards your final goal.

Walktalk: Fit kids and family fitness

Children sit in front of the television or computer screen for hours on end; they get out of breath walking up the stairs; they are always asking for a lift in the car rather than walking short distances; they lack the motivation to exercise and be active. Such complaints are often heard from parents these days.

In the light of increasing evidence that physical inactivity in children increases the risk of heart disease and obesity, it's important that parents take the lead and motivate their own families. And walking together is the easiest way to do this. Children who walk regularly will develop stamina, strength and flexibility gradually without strain or injury. Walking doesn't require any special equipment, and it can be done equally well by boys and girls. It's the one exercise that your kids can keep up for a lifetime.

And there are other benefits, too. Being outside in the open air allows you to spend some quality time together. Walking is one of the few physical activities that lets you concentrate as much on each other as on the exercise. Walking side by side is a non-confrontational way of opening up to others. What's the magic? It's likely that the natural rhythmic body action relaxes you and unlocks your emotions, enabling you to be more open with others. To coin a phrase: the family that walks together, talks together.

Footnotes

'Walking is an excellent exercise, available to everybody. I encourage regular family walks – at least a half an hour a day. It's a good way to spend time with your kids and a healthy habit.'
                                                    DR LEO GALLAND

DAY 22
30–35 minutes

warm-up	target zone	cool-down
walk slowly	walk briskly	walk slowly
5	20–25	5

Music to move by

Walking is a natural mood-elevator and promotes feelings of happiness and well-being: this is known as the 'walker's high'. That's partly because of the rhythmic action of walking itself which promotes increased confidence and a feeling of being in control. And it's partly because walking burns up stress hormones, which make us tense, and increases relaxation hormones called endorphins, which have a tranquillising effect and lift our mood. These beneficial effects are enhanced if we listen to music while we walk.

We know, from the work of music therapists, that music can take us from a highly tense state to a relaxed yet alert state in just a few minutes. Why? Surprise, surprise! It's endorphins again. It seems that music also triggers their release, making us feel less anxious. So, putting the two together, why not take a personal cassette player with you on your next walk and listen to music to match your stride and mood. Listen to a favourite tape, or buy one of the specialist walking tapes which help you to gradually increase your pace to the beat of the music – music with a fast beat if you want to maintain a brisk pace and soothing classical music for a meditative stroll. Tapes are available which cater for a wide range of musical tastes – pop, classical, country, swing and marches. It may be a good idea to avoid vocal pieces, which can be distracting.

It might seem obvious, but remember to look where you are going when listening to a music tape while on the move. Headphones can distract you from traffic or other dangers on the road, so if you're listening to music, look ahead and stay alert to your surroundings at all times.

Footnotes
'Music's the Medicine of the Mind.'   JOHN LOGAN (1744–88)

DAY 23
35 minutes

warm-up	target zone	cool-down
walk slowly	*walk briskly*	*walk slowly*
5	25	5

It's a shore thing

Turn off your television, turn off your computer and your mobile phone, and connect with yourself. Rediscover your calmer side with a brisk inner walk on the beach, and let the sound of the lapping waves lull you into a peaceful, meditative state. For as long as man can remember, water has been used as a symbol for our emotions. A wild and turbulent sea expresses agitation and anxiety, while waves gently lapping against the shore suggest calmness and tranquillity.

From morning to night our minds are bombarded with sensory events, from commuter crowds and traffic to telephones, television, voicemail and e-mail. When we make an effort to leave all this behind and just let go, our minds become calm and clear of the daily clutter. So relax, take an inner walk on the beach, and just go with the flow.

Walktalk: Can walking help arthritis?

According to rheumatologists, many people suffering from arthritis are able to benefit from regular exercise. And the safest exercise of all is walking. Walking helps to strengthen the muscles attached to the arthritic joints, and can relieve some of the pain when bones rub against bones. It may also prevent some joint inflammation. And the natural tranquil-lising effect of walking helps to ease arthritic pain through the release of endorphins. Their mood-elevating effect can also reduce the feelings of depression and lethargy often associated with arthritis. But be careful! Take it gently, rest frequently and don't walk through pain. Remember to warm up thoroughly first, walk only as far as feels comfortable, and increase the length of your walks gradually.

Make a point of discussing the problem with your doctor. It may be that your body needs the benefit of some additional strengthening and stretching exercises like those in the Bodywise section (see pages 132–42).

Footnotes
'The land of our better selves is most surely reached by walking.'
                                                    H. I. BROCK

DAY 24
0 minutes

rest day

With a little help from your friends

While it's possible to develop a regular walking habit on your own, it may be a lot easier to step out every day if you have a friend to keep you company. The hardest part of starting a new exercise programme is actually keeping it up week in, week out, and it can be so much easier if you have someone to support you and keep you motivated. Look for a walking partner or partners among family, friends and colleagues at work. They don't have to join you on every walk, but perhaps one day you could walk to work with a friend and another day take a refreshing walk during your lunch hour. Your walks will become a lot more interesting and provide a way of sharing conversation with other like-minded people.

If you cannot find a walking companion within your immediate circle of friends and family members, consider seeking one out. You could put a notice on the bulletin board at your local health and fitness centre or at your workplace. Or you could simply take the initiative and start your own walking group by advertising the time and place you intend to meet. You may be surprised how many other people are only too willing to join you!

In step with your daily rhythms

The Chinese philosopher Chuang Tzu said: 'The true man breathes with his heels.' Why? Because walking is as natural as breathing. The alternating rhythmic motion of the arms and legs – left, right, left, right; one, two, one, two – is similar to the inhalation and exhalation of the lungs when we breathe. To connect with these natural rhythms, centre your awareness in your body as it moves through the air, and feel the spring of your heel and toes as each step propels you forward.

Footnotes

'Come walk with me.'   EMILY BRONTË

DAY 25
35 minutes

warm-up	target zone	cool-down
walk slowly	walk briskly	walk slowly
5	25	5

Connect with yourself

When you want to get a clearer perspective on life, head for open spaces and connect with your spirit. The relentless pace of modern life often dulls our senses and divorces us from our real selves. Nature and open spaces widen our perception and enable us to see ourselves and the world around us in a new light. It's no accident that Buddhist temples are often situated on hillsides, which can provide a wide view of the countryside and a feeling of energy and expansiveness. So head for the hills and mountain tracks and commune a little with nature's healing energies.

Walktalk: Walking and high blood pressure

Overweight, overworked, overstressed and a sedentary lifestyle: this is the typical image of a person with high blood pressure, or hypertension. Yet the truth is that high blood pressure affects people of all ages, races, social classes, sizes and shapes, men and women, even children. Although antihypertensive drugs are widely prescribed, exercise is an alternative option for mild hypertension. Studies by physicians and exercise physiologists have concluded that exercise can be a potent tool for lowering blood pressure.

Regular aerobic walking can help by making the heart work more efficiently and by improving the circulation. Blood vessels become more elastic and the delivery of oxygen to the tissues is increased.

People who have high blood pressure may also be overweight, and studies confirm that blood pressure can be reduced by weight loss. Regular aerobic walking, combined with the low-fat, high-fibre diet outlined in the 30-Day Healthy-Eating Plan, is an excellent way of losing weight.

Anyone with hypertension should not hesitate to take medication prescribed by their doctor. But for mild hypertension, lifestyle changes such as exercise, reducing stress, and improving diet (healthy eating, watching your weight and cutting down on salt, alcohol and tobacco) may be just the ticket.

Footnotes

'Where even the motion of an angel's wing
Would interrupt the intense tranquillity
Of silent hills, and more than silent sky.'

WILLIAM WORDSWORTH

DAY 26
35–40 minutes

warm-up	target zone	cool-down
walk slowly	walk briskly	walk slowly
5	25–30	5

Exercising your options

Although fitness walking, combined with a regular routine of
stretching and strengthening exercises, will keep your body fit
and healthy, you may wish to use other aerobic activities to
add variety to your normal routine. As a low-intensity, low-
impact exercise, fitness walking is an excellent foundation
exercise, but as your fitness improves, you may wish to add
other forms of aerobic exercise such as swimming, cycling and
low-impact aerobics.

Combining different activities provides your body with a
type of cross-training. This means that instead of focusing on
one activity, you 'cross over' and add others into your
schedule. This can boost fitness gains and overall conditioning
more effectively than simply sticking with one activity. Because
each activity conditions and exercises muscle groups in
different ways, the chance of suffering pulled muscles or other
injuries is reduced. And activities tend to complement each
other in helping to build overall stamina, strength and
suppleness.

Exercising your options in this way will make your
workouts more interesting and variable. Some days, for
instance, you could cycle to work, walk during the lunch hour,
and take a swim in the evening. Or mix and match activities
during the week to suit your personal preference and to ensure
that, above all, you have some fun.

Take a walk on the wild side

'Coming over the stile and into the grove one felt immediately
a great sense of peace and stillness. Not a thing was moving. It
seemed sacrilegious to walk through it, to tread the ground . . .
the great redwood trees were absolutely still . . . you stood still
hardly daring to breathe.' This is how Krishnamurti, the
mystic, describes a walk in the woods in his journal.

There's an intimacy and an immediacy about being
surrounded by trees and leaves and the smell of damp earth.
So take a walk on the wild side. Connect with nature and your
own natural rhythms, and preserve your health and your
spirits while wandering through woods free from worldly
cares.

Footnotes

'Life consists with wildness. The most alive is the wildest. Not
yet subdued to man, its presence refreshes him.'

HENRY DAVID THOREAU

DAY 27
35–40 minutes

warm-up	target zone	cool-down
walk slowly	*walk briskly*	*walk slowly*
5	25–30	5

A brisk walk to beat the blues

In the doldrums? Feeling depressed? At a low ebb? Instead of
reaching for alcohol or anti-depressants, try getting outside in
the open air and taking a brisk walk. For years we've known

that our minds affect our bodies, but it's only recently that we've come to understand how much our bodies affect our minds. Various studies suggest that people who are depressed feel much better after regular exercise. And the scientific studies are borne out by a survey carried out in the United States by *Walking* magazine which found that for 98 per cent of readers, a primary reason for walking was to feel good afterwards.

Exercise juices up our system with endorphins, the feel-good hormones. These morphine-like chemicals help suppress pain and elevate mood, and physical activity increases their level. Studies also show that regular exercise helps the body burn off stress hormones such as cortisol, which is found in abnormally high levels in stressed individuals. So it seems that walking really can help chase away the blues. Here are just a few ways to use walking to lift your mood:

Plan ahead. Motivate yourself by visualising how much better you will feel when you get back from a refreshing, bad-mood-busting walk.

Begin with deep breaths. Before you start out, take some deep breaths to help relax your mind and body. Once you begin moving, your breathing will deepen naturally.

Think and feel positive. Therapists say that simply adopting a positive state of mind can help lift depression. So walk briskly with a smile on your face and look the world right in the eye. You will feel so much better.

Be aware of tension. Be aware of hunched-up shoulders. Keep your shoulders back and down and relaxed, with your arms swinging naturally.

Share the load. Walk the talk: take a caring friend along with you, someone who will listen without judging or giving advice.

Footnotes

'Sit as little as possible. Give no credence to any thought that
was not born outdoors while one moved about freely.'

FRIEDRICH WILHELM NIETZSCHE

DAY 28
35–40 minutes

warm-up	target zone	cool-down
walk slowly	*walk briskly*	*walk slowly*
5	25–30	5

Common ground

The historian G. M. Trevelyan said, 'Walking is a land of many
paths and no paths, where everyone goes his own way and is
right.' Although walking evokes a different response in
different people, for centuries writers, poets and philosophers
have all been great walkers and have praised the virtues of
walking.

Shakespeare, Samuel Johnson, Boswell, Robert Louis
Stevenson, Jane Austen and Charles Darwin were great
walkers. Thoreau, Emerson, Abraham Lincoln and Albert
Einstein walked for pleasure and recreation. The poets Shelley,
Keats and De Quincey all walked regularly, as did Wordsworth
and Coleridge. Balzac, Rousseau and Nietzsche all praised the
benefits of walking. The French novelist Gustave Flaubert
always took long walks before sitting down to write, and
William Hazlitt, the essayist, said that walking gave him 'a
little breathing space'. Enthusing about the delights of
perambulation, he said, 'Give me the clear blue sky over my
head . . . a winding road before me . . . I laugh, I sing for joy.'
And Honoré de Balzac, the French writer, echoed the same

thoughts when he said of walking, 'This first taste of freedom, physically experienced through the leg muscles, brought an indescribable alleviation to my soul.'

Hippocrates, the father of medicine, prescribed walks to all his patients. Plato, the great Greek philosopher, expounded his philosophy while walking up and down an olive grove in Athens some 2400 years ago. And Plato's pupil Aristotle discoursed with his students while walking, and founded the Peripatetic School of Philosophy.

Give some thought today to all those fellow walkers who have loved and praised the joys of walking. And end the day by reading some inspiring thoughts from a few of them. Let Wordsworth inspire you with the elevated thoughts of 'Tintern Abbey', or dip into a writer like Thoreau whose essay 'Walking' is a classic of walking literature. These writings will motivate you and they make excellent reading.

Footnotes

'Such blessing is there in perfect liberty.'

SAMUEL TAYLOR COLERIDGE

DAY 29
40 minutes

warm-up	target zone	cool-down
walk slowly	*walk briskly*	*walk slowly*
5	30	5

Taking steps to stop headaches

A dull, tight squeezing pain around the forehead, the scalp and the back of the neck – do you recognise the feeling?
Headaches are a major cause of time lost at work, and just

about everyone suffers from them at one time or another. Although there are many types of headaches, muscle contraction or 'tension' headaches are the most common.

To escape from the grip of tension headaches, the first solution is to pay attention to the sources of the stress causing the headaches in order to prevent them recurring. But once the vice tightens around your head, instead of reaching for a couple of painkillers, try some exercise to relieve your suffering.

'People who walk briskly or jog have reported dramatic improvements in their headaches,' say Alan Rapoport and Fred Sheftell, two physicians who run the New England Center for Headaches in the United States. 'By making changes in your diet, your exercise patterns, and your ways of dealing with stress, you can substantially reduce and prevent headache pain.' How does walking help?

- It improves breathing, which in turn induces relaxation, improves circulation, and increases the oxygen in the blood stream
- It releases endorphins, those pain-relieving chemicals in the brain which create a positive mood change
- It makes the liver more efficient and more able to flush out toxins from the blood that irritate nerves and cause pain
- It improves posture by strengthening muscles around the spine

As you walk, focus on your posture and your tense areas. Walk tall, with your head up and shoulders back. Then loosen up your shoulders with a few gentle rolls and feel the tension in your neck gradually relax. As you step into a brisk pace, your relaxed, positive mood will clear the air and clear your head.

Footnotes
Stall headaches before they strike by getting plenty of sleep. And drink lots of water to prevent dehydration, an unsuspected headache trigger.

DAY 30
40 minutes

warm-up	target zone	cool-down
walk slowly	*walk briskly*	*walk slowly*
5	30	5

Keeping up the momentum

'The easiest way to change yourself is physically . . . physical change is quick,' says American fitness expert Dr George Sheehan. Yet hard-won gains in health, fitness, increased energy and weight loss can easily be cancelled out if you don't keep up your exercise programme.

You can miss the odd day, even a couple of days here and there, and it won't make a lot of difference, but if you don't keep up your regular programme of aerobic walking, combined with stretching and strengthening exercises, any gains will be quickly cancelled out. But that's not going to happen to you, is it?

As you finish your 30-Day Plan, not only will you be fitter, slimmer and more energetic, but you will have taken a major step forward in building an exercise routine which you can keep up for a lifetime. So keep on walking and eating healthily: follow the example of the Healthy-Eating Pyramid (see page 79) and continue to use the recipes in the Healthy-Eating Plan.

Many of us begin a new exercise routine such as aerobic walking to get fit and lose weight. But very quickly we discover that walking is about much more than this. Remember what the readers of *Walking* magazine said: 98 per cent walked regularly because it made them feel good. When it comes down to it, we walk because it makes us feel good, and as an added bonus it keeps us fit and healthy and keeps our weight down. And that's why it's easy to keep up, year in, year out. Plus the fact that it's easy, it's safe, it costs very little, and we can walk alone or with our friends or family and spend some quality time with them. Walking is, quite simply, the best exercise.

Footnotes

'I travel not to go anywhere, but to go.'

ROBERT LOUIS STEVENSON

The Walker's Diet

THE 30-DAY HEALTHY-EATING AND WEIGHT-LOSS PLAN

'"How long does getting thin take?" Pooh asked anxiously.'

A. A. MILNE

Imagine for a few moments that you are walking through an open-air food market on a warm summer's day. The fruit and vegetable stalls are brimming over with fresh foods that are practically inviting you to eat them. Red and green peppers and purple aubergines glisten in the sun; onions, garlic and olives are bursting with flavour; there are bunches of fresh basil and parsley, ripe peaches and nectarines and juicy lemons and oranges.

It is these foods that make us think of energy and vitality, and of delicious, nutritious meals. Fresh fruit and vegetables are not only easy to prepare; they are also versatile. In The Walker's Diet you can see how vegetables can be an integral part of a meal, playing a major role, rather than just being something added at the side of the plate. And the recipes can easily be adapted to include the kinds of fish, meat or vegetables available if any of the ingredients are out of season or you don't like a particular food.

The Walker's Diet takes a balanced, moderate approach to eating. The easiest way to eat healthily and lose weight naturally is to follow the guidelines of the Healthy-Eating Pyramid, as recommended in the UK, in the United States and by the World Health Organisation. You can see which foods you should eat more of and which should be eaten in smaller quantities. The Pyramid shows the main food groups and the recommended daily quantities of each group. By eating more of the foods at the base of the Pyramid and less of the foods towards the top, you will enjoy a healthier diet and increased energy and vitality.

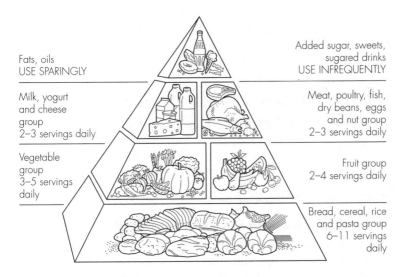

Fats, oils
USE SPARINGLY

Added sugar, sweets,
sugared drinks
USE INFREQUENTLY

Milk, yogurt
and cheese
group
2–3 servings daily

Meat, poultry, fish,
dry beans, eggs
and nut group
2–3 servings daily

Vegetable
group
3–5 servings
daily

Fruit group
2–4 servings daily

Bread, cereal, rice
and pasta group
6–11 servings
daily

A well-balanced diet is the key to health, vitality and successful weight control. Every day we need to ensure that our meals contain all the essential nutrients: carbohydrates, protein, fat, vitamins, minerals and water. In Further Food Facts for Fitness Walkers (see page 191), we shall take a look at each of these nutrients, as well as other aspects of nutrition.

When following The Walker's Diet, sometimes you may prefer to have the Main Meal at lunchtime and the Light Meal in the evening. The meals are designed to fit in with your own lifestyle; many of the Light Meals are suitable to be packed in a lunch box for you to take to work.

The recipes are suitable for all the family and can be followed if you are entertaining friends. When you have completed 30 days of The Walker's Diet, you will realise how easy it is to make a balanced, nutritious diet part of your daily life. To maintain your feelings of energy and vitality, continue using the recipes or adapt some of your favourites. Nutritious and delicious foods really can be part of a long-term plan to maintain health, fitness and vitality.

The Walker's Diet Breakfasts

Studies show that people who eat a nutritious breakfast are better able to cope with the stresses and strains of the day ahead. The suggestions here are for one person.

Start the day with the juice of half a lemon squeezed into hot water.

Plus your choice of fruit juice from the following (freshly juiced when possible):

> orange, grapefruit, apple, cranberry, prune

and one piece of fruit (the following are suggestions from which to make your choice):

> apple, orange, peach, nectarine, mango,
> papaya, grapefruit, prunes

and your choice from the following:

- porridge (made with semi-skimmed milk) with 5 ml (1 tsp) clear honey
- bowl of home-made muesli with semi-skimmed milk
- bowl of bran flakes with semi-skimmed milk
- poached egg on a toasted wholemeal muffin
- boiled egg with a slice of wholemeal toast
- slices of grilled tomato on a toasted wholemeal muffin
- grilled mushrooms with a slice of wholemeal toast
- lean slice of cooked ham with tomato wedges and a slice of wholemeal bread
- 50 g (2 oz) grated cheese melted on wholemeal toast with slices of grilled tomato
- large slice of wholemeal toast with 10 ml (2 tsp) marmalade or jam

The recipes for Light Meals and Main Meals are for two people. Simply halve or double the quantities according to how many people you are cooking for. Pack the Light Meal in a lunch box if you are at work during the day; if the meal is not suitable for a lunch box, use a recipe from another day that balances well with the Main Meal. Eat fresh fruit and/or low-fat yogurt as a dessert after Main Meals.

DAY 1

Breakfast

Make your choice from The Walker's Diet Breakfasts

Light Meal

Tuna and Leek Salad
200 g (7oz) tin tuna
2 medium leeks
10 ml (2 tsp) olive oil
5 ml (1 tsp) balsamic vinegar
4 brazil nuts
freshly ground black pepper
2 lemon wedges

Trim the leeks and cut in half widthways. Lightly cook in boiling salted water then drain thoroughly and allow to cool. Drain and flake the tuna. Arrange the leeks on serving plates and scatter the tuna on top. Mix together the olive oil and balsamic vinegar and spoon over the tuna and leeks. Finely slice the brazil nuts and scatter over the salad. Add some freshly ground pepper and garnish with the lemon wedges. Serve with crusty bread.

Main Meal

Penne with Roasted Vegetables
150 g (6 oz) penne pasta
1 medium red onion
1 medium aubergine
2 medium courgettes
1 small red pepper
1 small green pepper
100 g (4 oz) mushrooms
4 medium tomatoes
15 ml (1 tbsp) fresh basil leaves
chilli sauce, to taste
freshly ground sea salt and black pepper
8 black olives

Put the onion, aubergine, courgettes and red and green peppers, all left whole, on to a baking tray and roast in a preheated oven, Gas Mark 6 (200°C/400°F), for about 30 minutes, turning the vegetables twice. Add the mushrooms and tomatoes and cook for a further 10 minutes. Remove the tray from the oven and allow the vegetables to cool slightly so that they can be handled. Loosely wrap the red and green peppers in some clingfilm to help loosen the skin. Trim the onion, aubergine and courgettes, then cut into bite-size pieces. Remove the skin from the red and green peppers and the tomatoes by making an incision in the skin and gently peeling it away, then discard it. Cut the peppers, tomatoes and mushrooms into small pieces. Cook the penne as directed, then drain. While the pasta is cooking, put all the vegetables into another large pan and add the basil (torn into small pieces), chilli sauce and some freshly ground salt and pepper. Add half a small glass of cold water, stir and heat the vegetables thoroughly, adding a little more water if necessary. Arrange the penne on serving plates and spoon the roasted vegetables over the pasta. Garnish with the black olives and serve with a green salad.

DAY 2

Breakfast

Make your choice from The Walker's Diet Breakfasts

Light Meal

Feta and Tomato Pitta
75 g (3 oz) feta cheese
2 medium tomatoes
wedge of cucumber
small bunch of watercress
2 pitta breads
freshly ground black pepper

Thinly slice the feta cheese, tomatoes and cucumber. Prise open
the pitta bread to form an envelope and put a layer of watercress
into the pitta bread. Arrange the slices of feta cheese, tomato and
cucumber on the watercress and add some freshly ground black
pepper. Gently press the pitta bread closed and slice in half diagonally to serve.

Main Meal

Chicken Dhansak
2 chicken breast fillets
1 medium onion
2 cloves garlic
150 g (6 oz) mushrooms
420 g (15 oz) tin cooked lentils
125 ml (5 fl oz) low-fat natural yogurt
10 ml (2 tsp) ground coriander
5 ml (1 tsp) ground cumin
5 ml (1 tsp) chilli sauce
10 ml (2 tsp) safflower oil (or other vegetable oil)
freshly ground sea salt

Remove the skin from the chicken and discard it and cut the meat into thin strips. Slice the onion, garlic and mushrooms. Drain the cooked lentils. Heat the oil in a large pan and add the onion, garlic and chicken strips and cook over a medium heat, stirring to prevent sticking, for about 10 minutes, adding a little water if necessary. Stir in the coriander, cumin and chilli sauce. Add the mushrooms and some freshly ground salt and cook for a further 5 minutes. Stir in the lentils and the yogurt and heat thoroughly. Serve with basmati rice, cooked as directed.

DAY 3

Breakfast

Make your choice from The Walker's Diet Breakfasts

Light Meal

Italian Salad
1 small avocado
1 mozzarella cheese
2 medium tomatoes
10 ml (2 tsp) fresh basil
8 black olives
freshly ground black pepper
2 lemon wedges

Peel and thinly slice the avocado and slice the mozzarella cheese and the tomatoes. Arrange the avocado, mozzarella and tomato slices on serving plates. Tear the basil leaves into small pieces and scatter over the salad. Add the olives and some freshly ground pepper and garnish with the lemon wedges. Serve with wholemeal bread.

Main Meal

Mackerel with Provençal Vegetables
2 large mackerel fillets
4 shallots
2 cloves garlic
2 medium courgettes
1 small fennel bulb
420 g (15 oz) tin tomatoes
10 ml (2 tsp) Nam Pla fish sauce
5 ml (1 tsp) fresh thyme
freshly ground sea salt and black pepper

Slice the shallots, garlic and courgettes. Trim the fennel and cut into small pieces. Put the shallots, garlic and fennel in a large pan with the tomatoes and cook over a medium heat for about 10 minutes, stirring to prevent sticking. Add the courgettes, fish sauce, thyme and some freshly ground salt and pepper and mix thoroughly. Lay the mackerel fillets, skin side up, on top of the vegetables and cover the pan. Cook for a further 10 minutes. Remove the skin from the fish if desired, then serve the mackerel on top of the vegetables with a jacket potato.

DAY 4

Breakfast

Make your choice from The Walker's Diet Breakfasts

Light Meal

Ham and Watercress Sandwich
2 slices lean cooked ham
small bunch watercress
10 ml (2 tsp) low-fat mayonnaise
5 ml (1 tsp) mustard
4 thin slices wholemeal bread

Mix together the mayonnaise and mustard and spread on to the slices of bread. Arrange the watercress on two slices of bread and lay the ham on top of the watercress. Make up the sandwiches and cut into triangles. Serve with tomato wedges.

Main Meal

Pepper Tortilla
1 small red pepper
1 small green pepper
2 shallots
5 ml (1 tsp) fresh parsley
4 large eggs
30 ml (2 tbsp) milk
10 ml (2 tsp) safflower oil
freshly ground sea salt and black pepper

Finely slice the red and green peppers and the shallots. Heat the oil in a large frying pan and cook the peppers and shallots over a medium heat for about 5 minutes. Lightly whisk the eggs with the milk and some freshly ground salt and pepper. Chop the parsley and add to the eggs. Pour the eggs over the peppers and cook until almost set. Put under a preheated grill for a few moments to brown the top. Serve immediately with a green salad and crusty bread.

DAY 5

Breakfast

Make your choice from The Walker's Diet Breakfasts

Light Meal

Roasted Sweet Potato with Tuna Mayonnaise
2 small sweet potatoes
200 g (7 oz) tin tuna

2 spring onions
10 ml (2 tsp) low-fat mayonnaise
freshly ground black pepper

Bake the potatoes until they feel soft to the touch, then split them lengthways. Meanwhile, drain and flake the tuna. Finely slice the spring onions. Mix together the tuna, spring onions and mayonnaise and spoon on to the sweet potatoes. Add some freshly ground pepper.

Main Meal

Spicy Beef
220 g (8 oz) fillet or rump steak
1 medium red onion
1 clove garlic
4 medium tomatoes
1 small red pepper
1 small green pepper
100 g (4 oz) mushrooms
1 small tin cooked red kidney beans, drained
chilli sauce, to taste
10 ml (2 tsp) safflower oil
freshly ground sea salt and black pepper

Cut the steak into slivers. (This is more easily done if the steak has been in the freezer for 20–30 minutes.) Slice the onion, garlic, red and green peppers and mushrooms and chop the tomatoes. Put the onion, garlic, tomatoes and chilli sauce into a large pan with half a cup of water and cook over a medium heat for 10 minutes, stirring occasionally. Add the red and green peppers and mushrooms and cook for a further 5 minutes. Meanwhile, heat the safflower oil in a frying pan and add the steak, stirring to prevent sticking. Cook for about 5 minutes. Add the cooked red kidney beans to the vegetables and heat thoroughly. Stir the steak into the vegetables and add freshly ground salt and pepper. Serve with brown rice and braised shredded cabbage.

DAY 6

Breakfast

Make your choice from The Walker's Diet Breakfasts

Light Meal

Spring Salad
4 asparagus spears
100 g (4 oz) petits pois
2 medium tomatoes
wedge of cucumber
salad leaves
50 g (2 oz) pine nuts
5 ml (1 tsp) olive oil
5 ml (1 tsp) white wine vinegar
freshly ground black pepper
2 lemon wedges

Break the woody ends from the asparagus and discard. Lightly cook the asparagus and the petits pois and toast the pine nuts, then leave to cool. Slice the tomatoes and cucumber. Arrange the salad leaves on serving plates, then add the tomato and cucumber slices and the petits pois and place the asparagus spears on top. Scatter the pine nuts over the salad. Mix together the olive oil and white wine vinegar and drizzle the dressing over the salad. Add some freshly ground pepper and garnish with the lemon wedges. Serve with wholemeal bread.

Main Meal

Bucatini with Smoked Salmon and Prawns
150 g (6 oz) bucatini (or spaghetti)
4 shallots
100 g (4 oz) button mushrooms
75 g (3 oz) smoked salmon

125 g (5 oz) prawns
125 ml (5 fl oz) low-fat single cream
10 ml (2 tsp) Nam Pla fish sauce
3 ml (½ tsp) mustard
10 ml (2 tsp) fresh dill
freshly ground black pepper

Cook the pasta as directed, then drain. Meanwhile, slice the shallots and mushrooms and put in a medium pan with 125 ml (5 fl oz) water. Cook the shallots and mushrooms over a medium heat for about 5 minutes, reducing the liquid to about 5 ml (1 tsp). Cut the smoked salmon into small strips, peel the prawns and chop the dill. Add the prawns, cream, fish sauce, mustard and dill to the pan. After about 3 minutes, stir in the smoked salmon and add some freshly ground pepper. Put the pasta on serving plates and spoon the sauce over it, then serve immediately.

DAY 7

Breakfast

Make your choice from The Walker's Diet Breakfasts

Light Meal

Roast Peppers with Almonds
1 large red pepper
1 large green pepper
5 ml (1 tsp) olive oil
5 ml (1 tsp) balsamic vinegar
50 g (2 oz) split almonds
freshly ground black pepper

Put the red and green peppers, left whole, on a baking tray and roast in a preheated oven, Gas Mark 6 (200°C/400°F), for 30–40 minutes, turning them twice. Remove the tray from the oven and allow the peppers to cool slightly so that they can be handled. Loosely wrap them in some clingfilm to help loosen the skin. Remove the skin and discard. Cut the peppers into four pieces each, discarding the seeds but retaining the juices. Arrange on serving plates. Mix the olive oil and balsamic vinegar and dribble over the pepper salad. Lightly toast the almonds and scatter over the peppers. Add some freshly ground pepper. Serve with wholemeal bread.

Main Meal

Turkey Lombattini
2 125 g (5 oz) turkey breast fillets
2 shallots
100 g (4 oz) mushrooms
125 ml (5 fl oz) white wine
15 ml (1 tbsp) lemon juice
chilli sauce, to taste
5 ml (1 tsp) mustard
10 ml (2 tsp) fresh basil
freshly ground sea salt and black pepper

Put the turkey into an ovenproof dish. Thinly slice the shallots and mushrooms and scatter over the turkey. Mix together the white wine, lemon juice, chilli sauce and mustard with 125 ml (5 fl oz) water, then pour over the turkey. Cover and cook in a preheated oven, Gas Mark 6 (200°C/400°F), for 25 minutes. Tear the basil leaves into small pieces and add to the turkey and add some freshly ground salt and pepper. Cook uncovered for a further 5 minutes, adding a little more wine if necessary. Serve with new potatoes and broccoli.

DAY 8

Breakfast

Make your choice from The Walker's Diet Breakfasts

Light Meal

Frisée and Parma Ham Salad
frisée lettuce leaves
2 slices Parma ham
4 small mushrooms
5 ml (1 tsp) olive oil
5 ml (1 tsp) lemon juice
freshly ground black pepper

Mix together the oil and lemon juice. Finely slice the mushrooms and stir into the dressing. Arrange the frisée on individual plates and pour the mushrooms and dressing over the frisée. Cut the Parma ham into strips and scatter over the salad. Add some freshly ground pepper. Serve with crusty bread.

Main Meal

Seafood Jambalaya
150 g (6 oz) prawns
4 small squid
1 medium red onion
1 small red pepper
1 small green pepper
100 g (4 oz) mushrooms
100 g (4 oz) sweetcorn
5 ml (1 tsp) fresh parsley
10 ml (2 tsp) Nam Pla fish sauce
chilli sauce, to taste
10 ml (2 tsp) safflower oil
100 g (4 oz) basmati rice

freshly ground black pepper
2 lemon wedges

Cook the rice as directed. Peel the prawns and clean the squid and cut it into small pieces. Finely slice the onion, red and green peppers and mushrooms. Heat the oil in a large frying pan and cook the onion over a medium heat for 5 minutes, then add the peppers, mushrooms, sweetcorn, prawns and squid and cook for a further 5 minutes. Chop the parsley. Stir in the parsley, fish sauce and chilli sauce. Drain the rice and then add it to the vegetables and fish. Add some freshly ground pepper. Garnish with the lemon wedges and serve with a green salad.

DAY 9

Breakfast

Make your choice from The Walker's Diet Breakfasts

Light Meal

Salade Niçoise
small tin tuna in springwater
6 anchovy fillets
2 hard-boiled eggs
1 medium tomato
wedge of cucumber
2 shallots
lettuce leaves
10 ml (2 tsp) olive oil
10 ml (2 tsp) white wine vinegar
10 ml (2 tsp) lemon juice
freshly ground black pepper

Drain and flake the tuna, cut the hard-boiled eggs into quarters and thinly slice the tomato, cucumber and shallots. Put the lettuce leaves on serving plates and arrange all the other salad ingredients on the lettuce. Mix together the olive oil, white wine vinegar and lemon juice and spoon over the salad. Add some freshly ground pepper. Serve with wholemeal bread.

Main Meal

Mushroom Stroganoff
350 g (12 oz) mushrooms
4 shallots
2 cloves garlic
5 ml (1 tsp) mustard
125 ml (5 fl oz) white wine
10 ml (2 tsp) Nam Pla fish sauce
125 ml (5 fl oz) low-fat single cream
freshly ground black pepper

Slice the mushrooms and finely slice the shallots and garlic. Put them in a large pan with 125 ml (5 fl oz) water, cover and simmer for 5 minutes. Add the mustard, wine and fish sauce and cook uncovered for a further 5 minutes, reducing the liquid to about 15 ml (1 tbsp). Add the cream and some freshly ground pepper and heat thoroughly. Serve with a jacket potato and spinach.

DAY 10

Breakfast

Make your choice from The Walker's Diet Breakfasts

Light Meal

Capri Wrap
1 mozzarella cheese
1 medium tomato

10 ml (2 tsp) fresh basil
2 soft tortillas
freshly ground black pepper

Lay the tortillas flat on two plates. Slice the mozzarella into eight pieces and lay across the middle of the tortillas, not too close to the edges. Slice the tomato and lay on top of the cheese. Scatter the basil leaves over the mozzarella and tomato and add some freshly ground pepper. Roll up the tortilla wraps and slice each one diagonally into two pieces.

Main Meal

Moroccan Lamb
220 g (8 oz) lean lamb
1 medium red onion
2 cloves garlic
1 small green chilli
420 g (15 oz) tin cooked chick peas, drained
8 dried apricots
5 ml (1 tsp) fresh mint
10 ml (2 tsp) safflower oil
freshly ground sea salt and black pepper

Cut the lamb into thin strips and slice the onion and garlic. Remove the seeds from the chilli and discard, then slice the chilli finely. Heat the oil in a large pan and add the onion, garlic and chilli. Cook over a medium heat for 2–3 minutes then add the strips of lamb. Cook for about 8 minutes, stirring to prevent sticking. Add a little water if necessary. Cut the apricots into small pieces and slice the mint finely. Stir the chick peas, apricots and mint into the lamb and heat thoroughly. Add some freshly ground salt and pepper. Serve with couscous, cooked as directed, and a green salad.

DAY 11

Breakfast

Make your choice from The Walker's Diet Breakfasts

Light Meal

Guacamole with Crudités
1 small ripe avocado
juice of ½ lemon
chilli sauce, to taste
freshly ground black pepper
1 small carrot
½ small red pepper
½ small green pepper

Cut the avocado in half and remove the peel. Put the flesh in a bowl and mash with a fork until fairly smooth. Add the lemon juice, chilli sauce and some freshly ground pepper and mix thoroughly. Spoon on to serving plates. Cut the raw vegetables into strips and arrange next to the guacamole.

Main Meal

Cod with Balsamic Dressing
2 125 g (5 oz) cod fillets
1 medium onion
100 g (4 oz) mushrooms
10 ml (2 tsp) olive oil
15 ml (1 tbsp) balsamic vinegar
10 ml (2 tsp) lemon juice
10 ml (2 tsp) fresh parsley
freshly ground sea salt and black pepper

Chop the onion and mushrooms. Heat the oil in a medium pan and cook the onion for 5 minutes, stirring to prevent sticking.

Stir in the mushrooms, then put the cod fillets on top of the vegetables, cover and cook for 8–10 minutes, depending on the thickness of the fish. Chop the parsley. Add the balsamic vinegar, lemon juice, parsley and some freshly ground salt and pepper. Serve immediately with new potatoes and petits pois.

DAY 12

Breakfast

Make your choice from The Walker's Diet Breakfasts

Light Meal

Ham and Borlotti Bean Salad with Jacket Potato
2 medium baking potatoes
2 slices lean cooked ham
220 g (8 oz) tin cooked borlotti beans
2 spring onions
10 ml (2 tsp) low-fat mayonnaise
10 ml (2 tsp) low-fat natural yogurt
freshly ground black pepper

Bake the potatoes then split them lengthways. Meanwhile, cut the ham into small pieces and finely slice the spring onions, then put the ham and onions into a bowl with the beans. Mix the mayonnaise with the yogurt and add to the ham, beans and onions to coat them. Spoon the salad on to the potatoes and add some freshly ground pepper.

Main Meal

Penne Amalfi
150 g (6 oz) penne pasta
1 medium aubergine
1 medium onion

100 g (4 oz) mushrooms
4 medium tomatoes
4 anchovies
5 ml (1 tsp) capers
8 black olives
15 ml (1 tbsp) fresh basil
chilli sauce, to taste
freshly ground sea salt and black pepper

Cook the penne as directed, then drain. Meanwhile, peel the aubergine and cut into small pieces. Slice the onion and mushrooms and cut the tomato into small pieces. Put the vegetables into a pan with 250 ml (10 fl oz) water and cook over a medium heat for about 8 minutes. Cut the anchovies, capers and olives into small pieces and stir into the aubergine mixture. Tear the basil into small pieces then add the basil, chilli sauce and some freshly ground salt and pepper to the pan and stir well. Divide the penne on to individual plates, spoon over the sauce and serve immediately.

DAY 13

Breakfast

Make your choice from The Walker's Diet Breakfasts

Light Meal

Mexican Salad
100 g (4 oz) cooked peeled prawns
1 small avocado
2 spring onions
100 g (4 oz) sweetcorn
15 ml (1 tbsp) low-fat natural yogurt
15 ml (1 tbsp) lemon juice
2 iceberg lettuce leaves
freshly ground black pepper

Cut the avocado into small pieces and finely slice the spring onions. Put the avocado and onions in a bowl with the prawns, sweetcorn, yogurt and lemon juice and stir gently. Put the lettuce leaves on individual plates and spoon the salad into the leaves, then add some freshly ground pepper. Serve with wholemeal bread.

Main Meal

Chicken Florentine
2 chicken breast fillets
150 g (6 oz) fresh spinach
1 mozzarella cheese
10 ml (2 tsp) olive oil
juice of ½ lemon
10 ml (2 tsp) Nam Pla fish sauce
freshly ground black pepper

Remove the skin from the chicken and discard. Put the chicken into an ovenproof dish with the olive oil and lemon juice. Cover and cook in a preheated oven, Gas Mark 6 (200°C/400°F), for 20 minutes. Uncover the dish and cook for a further 5 minutes or until the chicken is cooked. Meanwhile, put the spinach in a pan with 30 ml (2 tbsp) water and cook over a medium heat for about 2 minutes. Drain thoroughly, then add the fish sauce to the spinach. Cut the mozzarella cheese into thin slices. When the chicken fillets are cooked, put them on a grill pan covered in foil. Arrange the spinach on top of the chicken and lay the slices of cheese on top of the spinach. Add some freshly ground pepper, then put under a preheated grill for about 2 minutes or until the cheese is browned. Serve immediately with a tomato, onion and basil salad.

DAY 14

Breakfast

Make your choice from The Walker's Diet Breakfasts

Light Meal

Couscous Salad with Grilled Peaches
100 g (4 oz) couscous
2 peaches
1 medium tomato
wedge of cucumber
1 small red onion
15 ml (1 tbsp) fresh mint
10 ml (2 tsp) lemon juice
10 ml (2 tsp) balsamic vinegar
freshly ground sea salt and black pepper

Prepare the couscous as directed and leave to cool. Meanwhile, halve the peaches and make two or three incisions into the flesh of the cut sides. Spoon the balsamic vinegar into the incisions and leave for about 10 minutes, then put the peaches under a preheated grill for 5 minutes. Leave to cool. Chop the tomato, cucumber, onion and mint and stir into the couscous. Add the lemon juice and some freshly ground salt and pepper. Spoon the couscous on to individual plates then add the grilled peaches. Garnish with a sprig of mint.

Main Meal

Swordfish with Greek Salad
2 125 g (5 oz) swordfish steaks
1 medium tomato
wedge of cucumber
75 g (3 oz) feta cheese
8 black olives

10 ml (2 tsp) olive oil
10 ml (2 tsp) white wine vinegar
2 lemon wedges
freshly ground black pepper

Brush the swordfish with some olive oil and cook under a pre-heated grill for about 10 minutes, turning so as to cook evenly. Add some freshly ground pepper halfway through cooking. Meanwhile, cut the tomato into wedges, slice the cucumber and crumble the feta. Gently mix them together, adding the black olives. Mix together the olive oil and white wine vinegar and spoon over the salad. Add some freshly ground pepper. Serve the swordfish, garnished with lemon wedges, with the Greek salad and new potatoes.

DAY 15

Breakfast

Make your choice from The Walker's Diet Breakfasts

Light Meal

Parma Ham and Mushroom Omelette
2 slices Parma ham
100 g (4 oz) mushrooms
5 ml (1 tsp) fresh parsley
4 large eggs
30 ml (2 tbsp) milk
10 ml (2 tsp) safflower oil
freshly ground sea salt and black pepper

Slice the mushrooms. Heat the oil in a large frying pan and cook the mushrooms over a medium heat for about 5 minutes. Lightly whisk the eggs with the milk and some freshly ground salt and pepper. Slice the Parma ham and chop the parsley and stir them into the eggs. Pour the eggs over the mushrooms and cook until almost set. Put under a preheated grill for a few moments to brown the top. Serve immediately with wholemeal bread.

Main Meal

Aubergine Galette
1 large aubergine
1 medium red onion
2 cloves garlic
100 g (4 oz) mushrooms
420 g (15 oz) tin chopped tomatoes
10 ml (2 tsp) Nam Pla fish sauce
1 mozzarella cheese
15 ml (1 tbsp) fresh basil
freshly ground black pepper

Cut the aubergine into 1-centimetre (⅜-inch) slices and arrange in a single layer in a large ovenproof dish. Slice the onion, garlic and mushrooms and arrange on top of the aubergine slices. Pour the tomatoes over the vegetables, cover the dish and bake in a preheated oven, Gas Mark 6 (200°C/400°F), for 30 minutes. Remove from the oven and sprinkle over the fish sauce. Cut the mozzarella into thin slices and arrange it on top of the aubergine, then add some freshly ground pepper. Put under a preheated grill for a few minutes until the mozzarella is golden. Tear the basil into small pieces and scatter over the galette. Serve with a green salad.

DAY 16

Breakfast

Make your choice from The Walker's Diet Breakfasts

Light Meal

Prawn and Watercress Pitta
150 g (6 oz) cooked prawns
small bunch of watercress
2 spring onions
5 ml (1 tsp) olive oil
5 ml (1 tsp) balsamic vinegar
freshly ground black pepper
2 pitta breads

Peel the prawns and shred the spring onions. Mix the olive oil and balsamic vinegar together in a bowl. Add the prawns, watercress, spring onions and some freshly ground pepper and mix to coat the salad with the dressing. Prise open the pitta bread to form an envelope. Spoon the salad into the pitta bread and gently press closed. Cut in half diagonally to serve.

Main Meal

Spaghetti Primavera
150 g (6 oz) spaghetti
220 g (8 oz) asparagus
4 shallots
2 cloves garlic
50 g (2 oz) pine nuts
50 g (2 oz) Parmesan cheese
15 ml (1 tbsp) fresh basil
125 ml (5 fl oz) low-fat single cream
freshly ground sea salt and black pepper

Cook the spaghetti as directed, then drain. Break the woody ends from the asparagus and discard, then cut the rest of the asparagus into 2.5-centimetre (1-inch) pieces. Finely slice the shallots and garlic and put them into a medium pan, add just enough water to cover and simmer for 5 minutes. Add the asparagus and cook for a further 5 minutes. Meanwhile, lightly toast the pine nuts and grate the Parmesan cheese. Reduce the cooking liquid to about 10 ml (2 tsp), then add the cream and heat through. Tear the basil into small pieces, then stir the basil, pine nuts and Parmesan cheese into the sauce and add some freshly ground salt and pepper. Serve the spaghetti on individual plates and spoon over the asparagus sauce.

DAY 17

Breakfast

Make your choice from The Walker's Diet Breakfasts

Light Meal

Roasted Sweet Potato with Sweetcorn Mayonnaise
2 small sweet potatoes
1 tin sweetcorn
2 spring onions
10 ml (2 tsp) low-fat mayonnaise
freshly ground black pepper

Bake the potatoes until soft to the touch, then split them length-ways. Meanwhile, drain the sweetcorn and finely slice the spring onions. Mix together the sweetcorn, spring onions and mayonnaise. Spoon on to the sweet potatoes and add some freshly ground pepper.

Main Meal

Pork Gitana
300 g (10 oz) pork fillet
1 medium red onion
1 small red pepper
1 small green pepper
100 g (4 oz) mushrooms
420 g (15 oz) tin chopped tomatoes
15 ml (1 tbsp) paprika
125 ml (5 fl oz) low-fat natural yogurt
freshly ground sea salt and black pepper

Cut the pork into bite-size pieces and slice the onion, red and green peppers and mushrooms. Put the pork and vegetables into a casserole with the tomatoes and paprika and cover. Cook in a preheated oven, Gas Mark 6 (200°C/400°F), for 1 hour. Add some freshly ground salt and pepper and cook uncovered for a further 15 minutes. Stir in the yogurt and allow to heat through for a few minutes. Serve with wholegrain rice and broccoli.

DAY 18

Breakfast

Make your choice from The Walker's Diet Breakfasts

Light Meal

Smoked Trout and Grape Salad
2 fillets smoked trout
small bunch grapes
small wedge of cucumber
lettuce leaves
15 ml (1 tbsp) low-fat natural yogurt
5 ml (1 tsp) creamed horseradish
freshly ground black pepper

Shred the lettuce leaves and arrange on individual plates. Mix the yogurt and horseradish in a medium bowl. Flake the smoked trout and finely slice the cucumber. Stir the trout, grapes and cucumber into the yogurt and horseradish. Spoon on to the lettuce leaves and add some freshly ground pepper. Serve with wholemeal bread.

Main Meal

Lentil Ragout

420 g (15 oz) tin cooked lentils
1 red onion
2 sticks celery
2 medium carrots
2 medium potatoes
15 ml (1 tbsp) tomato purée
125 ml (5 fl oz) red wine
15 ml (1 tbsp) Nam Pla fish sauce
125 ml (5 fl oz) low-fat natural yogurt
15 ml (1 tbsp) fresh parsley
freshly ground sea salt and black pepper

Cut the potatoes into cubes, put them in a small pan, cover with boiling water and simmer for 10–15 minutes or until cooked, then drain. Slice the onion, celery and carrots, put them in a large pan, cover with boiling water and simmer for about 10 minutes or until cooked. Reduce or drain the liquid to about 125 ml (5 fl oz). Drain the cooked lentils. Put the potatoes and the lentils into the large pan and stir in the tomato purée, red wine and fish sauce. Put back on the heat and mix thoroughly. Chop the parsley, then stir into the pan the yogurt, parsley and some freshly ground salt and pepper. Serve with braised shredded red cabbage.

DAY 19

Breakfast

Make your choice from The Walker's Diet Breakfasts

Light Meal

Spicy Egg Mayonnaise Sandwich
3 eggs
10 ml (2 tsp) low-fat mayonnaise
5 ml (1 tsp) chilli sauce
freshly ground sea salt and black pepper
4 thin slices wholemeal bread

Hard-boil the eggs and leave to cool, then peel. Put the eggs into a bowl and chop them finely. Add the mayonnaise, chilli sauce and salt and pepper and mix thoroughly. Make up the sandwiches with the wholemeal bread and cut into triangles. Serve with watercress.

Main Meal

Royal Indian Beef
300 g (10 oz) fillet or rump steak
1 medium red onion
2 small courgettes
100 g (4 oz) mushrooms
15 ml (1 tbsp) curry paste
75 g (3 oz) ground almonds
75 g (3 fl oz) low-fat single cream
10 ml (2 tsp) safflower oil
freshly ground sea salt and black pepper

Cut the steak into slivers. (This is more easily done if the steak has been in the freezer for 20–30 minutes.) Slice the onions, courgettes and mushrooms. Heat the oil in a large pan and cook the onions for 5 minutes, stirring to prevent sticking. Add the steak and cook for a further 5 minutes. Mix the curry paste with 125 ml (5 fl oz) boiling water and pour over the steak. Add the courgettes and mushrooms, cover the pan and cook for 10 minutes. Stir in the ground almonds and the cream and add some freshly ground salt and pepper. Serve with basmati rice.

DAY 20

Breakfast

Make your choice from The Walker's Diet Breakfasts

Light Meal

Bacon and Courgette Salad
4 rashers lean bacon
2 small courgettes
10 ml (2 tsp) olive oil
10 ml (2 tsp) balsamic vinegar
freshly ground black pepper
2 lemon wedges

Grill the bacon and leave to cool. Grate the courgettes. Heat the oil in a pan, add the grated courgettes and cook over a medium heat for about 8 minutes, stirring to prevent sticking, then leave to cool. Stir in the vinegar, then break the bacon into small pieces and mix with the courgettes. Spoon the salad on to individual plates and add some freshly ground pepper. Garnish with the lemon wedges and serve with crusty bread.

Main Meal

Salmon Pilaki
220 g (8 oz) fresh salmon fillet
1 medium onion

2 cloves garlic
4 medium tomatoes
small bunch celery leaves
125 ml (5 oz) fish stock
15 ml (1 tbsp) lemon juice
10 ml (2 tsp) fresh parsley
8 black olives
freshly ground sea salt and black pepper

Chop the onion, garlic, tomatoes and celery leaves and cook them in the fish stock over a medium heat for 10 minutes. Remove the skin from the salmon, then cook the salmon in the sauce for about 8 minutes, gently breaking it into pieces. Chop the parsley. Add the lemon juice, parsley and some freshly ground salt and pepper. Garnish with the black olives. Serve with new potatoes and cauliflower.

DAY 21

Breakfast

Make your choice from The Walker's Diet Breakfasts

Light Meal

Carrot and Celeriac Mayonnaise
2 medium carrots
wedge of celeriac
15 ml (1 tbsp) low-fat mayonnaise
10 ml (2 tsp) lemon juice
15 ml (1 tbsp) fresh basil
freshly ground black pepper

Grate the carrots and celeriac. Mix together the mayonnaise and lemon juice in a large bowl and add the grated carrots and celeriac. Stir to coat the vegetables with the dressing. Spoon on to individual plates and add some freshly ground pepper. Tear the basil into small pieces and scatter over the salad. Serve with wholemeal bread.

Main Meal

Turkey with Pine Nuts and Sultanas
2 125 g (5 oz) turkey breast fillets
1 red onion
100 g (4 oz) mushrooms
125 ml (5 fl oz) white wine
15 ml (1 tbsp) lemon juice
chilli sauce, to taste
75 g (3 oz) pine nuts
75 g (3 oz) sultanas
freshly ground sea salt and black pepper

Put the turkey into an ovenproof dish. Thinly slice the onion and mushrooms and scatter over the turkey. Mix together the white wine, lemon juice and chilli sauce and pour over the turkey. Cover and cook in a preheated oven, Gas Mark 6 (200°C/400°F), for 25 minutes. Add some freshly ground salt and pepper. Cook uncovered for a further 5 minutes, adding a little more wine if necessary. Toast the pine nuts and scatter them with the sultanas over the turkey. Serve with leek purée and petits pois.

DAY 22

Breakfast

Make your choice from The Walker's Diet Breakfasts

Light Meal

Herring with Jacket Potato
2 medium baking potatoes
4 small roll mop herrings

75 ml (3 fl oz) low-fat natural yogurt
small wedge of cucumber
freshly ground black pepper

Bake the potatoes, then split them lengthways. Cut the cucumber into fine slices and mix with the yogurt. Spoon the yogurt and cucumber into the potato and add some freshly ground pepper. Arrange the herrings next to the potato.

Main Meal

Spicy Vegetables with Couscous
1 medium aubergine
2 medium courgettes
1 small red pepper
1 small green pepper
1 red onion
2 cloves garlic
420 g (15 oz) tin chopped tomatoes
10 ml (2 tsp) Nam Pla fish sauce
chilli sauce, to taste
150 g (6 oz) couscous
freshly ground sea salt and black pepper

Prepare the couscous as directed. Peel the aubergine and cut into small pieces. Slice the courgettes, red and green peppers, onion and garlic. Put all the vegetables into a large pan with the tomatoes and cook over a medium heat for 10 minutes, stirring to prevent sticking. Add the fish sauce, chilli sauce and some freshly ground salt and pepper and cook for a further 5 minutes. Serve with the couscous.

DAY 23

Breakfast

Make your choice from The Walker's Diet Breakfasts

Light Meal

Asparagus and Egg Mayonnaise
8 asparagus spears
2 eggs
10 ml (2 tsp) low-fat mayonnaise
10 ml (2 tsp) lemon juice
freshly ground black pepper

Break the woody ends from the asparagus and discard. Lightly cook the asparagus and hard-boil the eggs, then leave both to cool. Mix together the mayonnaise and lemon juice. Peel the eggs and cut them in half and put them cut-side down on individual plates. Spoon the lemon mayonnaise over the eggs. Arrange the asparagus next to the eggs and add some freshly ground pepper. Serve with wholemeal bread.

Main Meal

Tuna Provençal
2 125 g (5 oz) tuna steaks
1 medium onion
2 cloves garlic
4 medium tomatoes
15 ml (1 tbsp) fresh basil
10 ml (2 tsp) olive oil
2 lemon wedges
freshly ground black pepper

Chop the onion, garlic and tomatoes and put them in a medium pan with about 30 ml (2 tbsp) water. Cook over a medium heat for 10 minutes, stirring to prevent sticking. Meanwhile, gently heat the olive oil in another pan and cook the tuna steaks for about 8 minutes, turning to cook evenly. Tear the basil into small pieces and stir into the sauce, adding some freshly ground pepper. Spoon the sauce on to serving plates and lay the tuna steaks on the sauce. Garnish with the lemon wedges. Serve with wholegrain rice and a green salad.

DAY 24

Breakfast

Make your choice from The Walker's Diet Breakfasts

Light Meal

Parma Ham and Avocado Wrap
2 slices Parma ham
1 small avocado
10 ml (2 tsp) fresh basil
2 soft tortillas
freshly ground black pepper

Lay the tortillas flat on two plates. Lay the Parma ham across the middle of the tortillas, not too close to the edges. Peel and slice the avocado and lay the slices on top of the Parma ham. Scatter the basil over the Parma ham and avocado and add some freshly ground pepper. Roll up the tortilla wraps and slice each one diagonally into two pieces to serve.

Main Meal

Courgette and Pepper Kebabs
2 small courgettes
1 small red pepper
1 small green pepper

1 medium red onion
8 cherry tomatoes
10 ml (2 tsp) olive oil
10 ml (2 tsp) balsamic vinegar
freshly ground black pepper

Cut the courgettes, onion and red and green peppers into bite-size pieces. If using wooden skewers, soak them in water for about 30 minutes to prevent them from burning during cooking. Make up kebabs with all the vegetables and lay them in a dish. Mix together the oil and vinegar and spoon over the vegetables, then add some freshly ground pepper. Leave to marinate for at least 30 minutes, turning occasionally to coat the kebabs in the marinade. Cook under a preheated grill for about 10 minutes, turning to prevent burning. Serve with new potatoes and a chicory and orange salad.

DAY 25

Breakfast

Make your choice from The Walker's Diet Breakfasts

Light Meal

Florentine Salad
2 eggs
100 g (4 oz) fresh spinach
10 ml (2 tsp) olive oil
10 ml (2 tsp) balsamic vinegar
8 black olives
freshly ground black pepper

Hard-boil the eggs and leave to cool, then peel and cut in half. Wilt the spinach leaves by putting them in a large pan with 15 ml (1 tbsp) boiling water and cooking over a medium heat for about 2 minutes. Drain and squeeze excess water from the leaves. Arrange the spinach on individual plates and place the eggs cut-side down on the spinach. Mix together the oil and balsamic vinegar and spoon over the eggs and spinach. Add some freshly ground pepper and garnish with the black olives. Serve with crusty bread.

Main Meal

Scampi Alfredo
300 g (10 oz) raw scampi
4 shallots
100 g (4 oz) small mushrooms
100 g (4 oz) petits pois
125 ml (5 fl oz) low-fat single cream
10 ml (2 tsp) Nam Pla fish sauce
10 ml (2 tsp) brandy
freshly ground black pepper

Finely slice the shallots and mushrooms. Put them in a medium pan with the petits pois and 125 ml (5 fl oz) boiling water. Bring back to the boil and simmer for 5 minutes. Add the scampi and cook for a further 5 minutes, then reduce the liquid to 5 ml (1 tsp). Stir in the cream and fish sauce and heat thoroughly. Add the brandy and some freshly ground pepper. Serve immediately with basmati rice.

DAY 26

Breakfast

Make your choice from The Walker's Diet Breakfasts

Light Meal

Smoked Mackerel Pâté
2 smoked mackerel fillets
125 g (5 oz) low-fat cottage cheese

10 ml (2 tsp) creamed horseradish
10 ml (2 tsp) lemon juice
freshly ground black pepper

Remove the skin from the smoked mackerel fillets and flake the fish. Put the cottage cheese into a bowl and crush it with a fork, making it as smooth as possible. Add the flaked fish, horseradish and lemon juice and mix thoroughly. Spoon on to individual plates and add some freshly ground pepper. Serve with wholemeal bread.

Main Meal

Chicken with Mango
2 chicken breast fillets
10 ml (2 tsp) curry paste
10 ml (2 tsp) low-fat natural yogurt
1 medium mango

Remove the skin from the chicken and discard. Score the chicken and put into an ovenproof dish. Mix the curry paste and natural yogurt and spread over the chicken as a marinade. Leave for at least half an hour (2–3 hours if possible). Put 30 ml (2 tbsp) of cold water into the base of the dish. Cover the chicken and bake in a preheated oven, Gas Mark 6 (200°C/400°F), for about 25 minutes. Uncover the dish and cook for a further 5 minutes. Meanwhile, cut the mango in half and remove the stone and peel. Cut each half into three or four slices. Preheat the grill and, during the last 5 minutes of cooking the chicken, grill the mango slices, turning so as to colour evenly. Serve with a jacket potato and sweetcorn.

DAY 27

Breakfast

Make your choice from The Walker's Diet Breakfasts

Light Meal

Ham, Apple and Cashew Nut Salad
2 slices lean cooked ham
1 medium apple
12 cashew nuts
10 ml (2 tsp) low-fat mayonnaise
juice of ½ lemon
lettuce leaves
freshly ground black pepper

Cut the ham into small pieces, thinly slice the apple and chop the cashew nuts. Mix together the mayonnaise and lemon juice in a bowl and add the ham, apple and nuts, stirring to coat with the lemon mayonnaise. Arrange the lettuce leaves on individual plates and spoon the salad on to the lettuce. Add some freshly ground pepper. Serve with crusty bread.

Main Meal

Bucatini Livornese
150 g (6 oz) bucatini (or spaghetti)
1 medium aubergine
1 medium red onion
100 g (4 oz) mushrooms
420 g (15 oz) tin tomatoes
1 mozzarella cheese
15 ml (1 tbsp) Nam Pla fish sauce
freshly ground black pepper

Cook the pasta as directed, then drain. Meanwhile, trim the aubergine and cut into cubes and slice the onion and mushrooms.

Put the aubergine and onion into a large pan with the tomatoes and cook over a medium heat for about 8 minutes, then add the mushrooms and fish sauce and cook for a further 5 minutes. Cut the mozzarella into small pieces and stir into the sauce, adding some freshly ground pepper. Put the pasta on serving plates and spoon over the sauce and serve immediately.

DAY 28

Breakfast

Make your choice from The Walker's Diet Breakfasts

Light Meal

Feta, Melon and Mint Salad
100 g (4 oz) feta cheese
½ small charentais melon (or melon of your choice)
wedge of cucumber
10 ml (2 tsp) fresh mint
15 ml (1 tbsp) low-fat natural yogurt
10 ml (2 tsp) lemon juice
freshly ground black pepper

Cut the feta into thin slices. Slice the melon and remove the skin, then arrange the melon and feta on individual plates. Cut the cucumber into very small pieces and chop the mint, then mix them together with the yogurt and lemon juice. Spoon over the salad and add some freshly ground pepper. Serve with wholemeal bread.

Main Meal

Agen Pork
300 g (10 oz) pork fillet
4 shallots
100 g (4 oz) mushrooms

15 ml (1 tbsp) olive oil
juice of ½ lemon
8 Agen prunes
10 ml (2 tsp) brandy
125 ml (5 fl oz) low-fat single cream
freshly ground sea salt and black pepper

Put the pork fillet in an ovenproof dish. Slice the shallots and mushrooms and scatter over the meat. Mix 10 ml (2 tsp) olive oil with the lemon juice and spoon over the pork. Cover the dish and cook in a preheated oven, Gas Mark 6 (200°C/400°F), for about 45 minutes. Slice the pork into medallions. Heat the rest of the olive oil in a pan. Put the pork medallions, shallots and mushrooms into the pan and cook for a further 5 minutes, adding any cooking juices. Cut the prunes into quarters and add to the meat. Add the brandy, cream and some freshly ground salt and pepper, stirring to prevent sticking. Serve with parsnip purée and mangetout.

DAY 29

Breakfast

Make your choice from The Walker's Diet Breakfasts

Light Meal

Sardines with Cannellini Bean Salad
6 fresh sardines
220 g (8 oz) tin cooked cannellini beans
2 spring onions
10 ml (2 tsp) low-fat mayonnaise
10 ml (2 tsp) low-fat natural yogurt
2 lemon wedges
freshly ground black pepper

Clean, gut and de-scale the sardines. (Many shops sell them ready to cook.) Cook under a preheated grill for about 10 minutes, turning to cook evenly. Meanwhile, finely slice the spring onions and put them into a bowl with the beans. Mix the mayonnaise with the yogurt, then add to the beans and onions and mix to coat them with the dressing. Place the sardines on serving plates and arrange the salad next to them. Add some freshly ground pepper. Garnish with the lemon wedges. Serve with crusty bread.

Main Meal

Aubergine and Mushroom Rogan Josh
1 large aubergine
220 g (8 oz) mushrooms
1 medium onion
15 ml (1 tbsp) rogan josh curry paste
125 ml (5 fl oz) low-fat natural yogurt
chilli sauce, to taste
freshly ground sea salt and black pepper

Trim the aubergine and cut into cubes. Slice the mushrooms and the onion. Put the aubergine, mushrooms and onion in a large pan with 300 ml (10 fl oz) boiling water. Simmer for 10 minutes, reducing the liquid to about 10 ml (2 tsp). Mix together the rogan josh paste and yogurt and add to the vegetables. Add some freshly ground salt and pepper. Cook for a further 5 minutes, adding chilli sauce to taste. Serve with basmati rice.

DAY 30

Breakfast

Make your choice from The Walker's Diet Breakfasts

Light Meal

Avocado and Orange Salad
1 small avocado
1 large orange
2 spring onions
8 black olives
freshly ground black pepper

Peel and slice the avocado and arrange on individual plates. Peel the orange and cut into segments, removing as much pith as possible. Squeeze the juice of two segments over the avocado, then arrange the other segments with the avocado. Finely slice the spring onions and scatter over the salad. Add some freshly ground pepper and garnish with the olives. Serve with wholemeal bread.

Main Meal

Beef with Leeks
300 g (10 oz) fillet or rump steak
2 medium leeks
10 ml (2 tsp) mustard
125 ml (5 fl oz) low-fat single cream
10 ml (2 tsp) olive oil
freshly ground sea salt and black pepper

Cut the steak into slivers. (This is more easily done if the steak has been in the freezer for 20–30 minutes.) Heat the oil in a frying pan and cook the steak for about 10 minutes. Meanwhile, finely slice the leeks, cover with boiling water and simmer in a large pan for about 8 minutes, then drain thoroughly. Mix the mustard and cream together and add to the steak, stirring to prevent sticking. Add some freshly ground salt and pepper. Arrange the leeks on serving plates and spoon the steak and sauce over them. Serve with new potatoes.

Bodywise

Stamina	is your ability to keep going without becoming too tired
Strength	is a measure of the force your muscles can produce
Suppleness	makes your body more flexible and keeps muscles and joints more mobile

Bodyfacts There are around 800 muscles in the human body.

Bodyfacts Did you know that you use over 200 different muscles when you walk?

SHAPING UP

Your level of fitness mirrors the efficiency of your heart, lungs and muscles. To be physically fit, your body requires stamina, strength and suppleness.

Stamina

As a low-risk exercise, brisk walking is the easiest and quickest way to develop stamina and endurance – or aerobic fitness. Walking works out almost every one of your body's large muscles, toning and strengthening your hips, thighs, stomach and buttocks, and also some of your shoulder muscles when you swing your arms. And if you increase the intensity of your workouts by adding hill walks, climbing flights of stairs, or simply walking faster, you will benefit from further gains in cardiovascular fitness. But to help you develop strength and suppleness, we have devised the Bodywise Workout for you to do twice a week (see over the page).

Strength

You've heard the saying 'Use it or lose it'. From the age of 30 onwards, most of us lose 3 to 6 per cent of our muscle mass each decade. That means less strength to perform tasks that we found easy in our youth: everything from lifting a heavy load or picking up a child to something as simple as removing a jar lid. Strength also helps to prevent injury. For example, strong back and abdominal muscles reduce the risk of back pain and chronic back problems. 'Basically, the difference between fit people and unfit people is not in their hearts and lungs,' says cardiologist and fitness expert George Sheehan. 'What you train is muscle, to get more miles per gallon by increasing its ability to metabolise oxygen.' Stronger muscles can also improve posture and physical appearance.

Your muscles are your metabolic engine. When your muscle mass decreases, your metabolism slows down and you store more calories as fat than you burn as fuel. By working out to build strong muscles, you raise your metabolic rate, increase your endurance and burn more calories. Since brisk walking itself is a fat-burning activity, then by both walking briskly (aerobically) and building strong muscles, you get the benefits of a double whammy. It's as simple as that.

Suppleness

Suppleness means flexibility: the ability to use your muscles and joints through the full potential range of their movement – bending, reaching, twisting and turning. As our modern sedentary existence tends to make us less active, it is easy to lose the flexibility in our muscles and joints. Combined with a decline in muscle strength, this means that our bodies become less able to cope with the demands we place upon them. Supple joints and muscles can also contribute to improved posture and physical appearance. And there is evidence to suggest that joints kept active and mobile are less likely to stiffen up in old age.

THE BODYWISE WORKOUT

'That which is used develops; that which is not used wastes away.'

HIPPOCRATES

The following exercises have all been designed to help you build strength and suppleness without straining yourself. The number of repetitions and the length of time suggested to hold the positions are only guidelines – if necessary, reduce these to a level you feel comfortable with.

If you are unfit or overweight and have little muscle tone or suppleness, then you should progress gradually with the exercises. Your movements should flow naturally and should never be forced to the point where they cause pain or discomfort.

Slowly stretch into each position, going only as far as is comfortable, hold for the required time, then come out of the position slowly. Aim to keep your breathing deep and natural throughout.

The Bodywise exercises that follow will complement your walking workout and will help tone and strengthen your body to cope with the demands of modern living. They will help you to control your weight and ease away stress, and you'll feel and look better, too.

Whenever you perform the Bodywise exercises as a stand-alone workout, be sure to complete the Bodywise Warm-Up which follows. But if you decide to do the Bodywise workout immediately after your walk, then complete your post-walk stretches as normal but omit the Bodywise Warm-Up, because walking has already warmed up your muscles. After your post-walk stretches, you can go straight into the Bodywise Strength and Tone exercises.

BODYWISE WARM-UP

Just as you should always warm up prior to fitness walking in the target zone, it's also necessary to warm up before your strength and tone workout: to increase blood flow, lubricate your joints and prepare your muscles for work. The following basic starting position will be used in many of the exercises to follow: stand with feet a little wider than hip-width apart, knees slightly bent and abdominals pulled in, and tighten and tuck bottom under to straighten back. (This is a pelvic tilt.)

1   Neck rolls

To release and relax the neck

Adopt basic starting position as described above and relax arms down by sides. Drop chin to chest and slowly roll head to one side (right ear towards right shoulder). Gently bring chin back to chest and repeat towards left shoulder. Repeat 3 times on each side, then bring chin back to chest and roll head up.

N.B. Never tilt head backwards – roll in a semicircle only.

2 Shoulder shrugs/circles

To mobilise and relax neck, shoulders and upper back

3 Arm raises

To loosen shoulders and upper back and increase oxygen flow

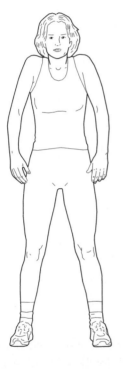

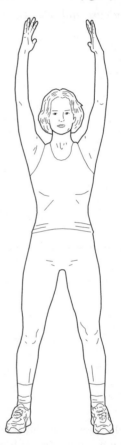

Stand as before, with arms relaxed by your sides. Lift and lower shoulders 6–8 times. Rotate shoulders forwards 6–8 times and rotate backwards 6–8 times.

Stand in basic position with arms by your sides. Inhale and slowly raise arms above head, then exhale and lower arms down. Repeat 6–8 times.

4   Ankle release

To increase ankle mobility

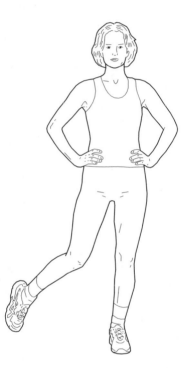

Slightly bend both knees. Place hands on hips (or hold on to a solid object for balance). Lift one foot off the floor and slowly circle one way then the other. Repeat with other foot.

5   Squats

To warm quadriceps

Stand in basic position but with feet wider apart and toes point-ing outwards. Slowly lower the bottom, bending knees out towards toes, going down for 2 counts, then rise up for 2 counts. Repeat 6–8 times. Then lower and lift for single counts, repeat-ing 6–8 times. Always keep hips above knee level.

6   Toe taps with arm raises

To increase blood flow and stretch waist and back

7   Hamstring curls

To warm and limber back of thighs

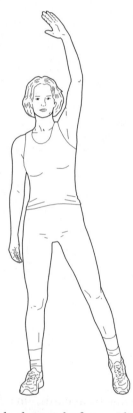

Shift body weight from side to side, tapping toes of alternate feet on floor. Add alternate arm raises (left arm, left toe, etc). This will increase the exercise intensity and stretch sides of body. Do 8 counts without arms and 8 counts with arms. Repeat twice.

Place hands on hips and keep head and chest up. Lift left foot towards left buttock and hold for 8 counts. Lower and repeat with right foot. Repeat twice with each foot.

8   Marching

To increase oxygen uptake and mobilise upper and lower body

9   Knee raises

To raise pulse rate and mobilise hips and upper body

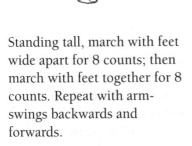

Standing tall, march with feet wide apart for 8 counts; then march with feet together for 8 counts. Repeat with arm-swings backwards and forwards.

Moving from narrow marching with steady breathing, keep back straight, abdominals in, and lift alternate knees up to hip level. Allow arms to swing naturally. Do 8 lifts and repeat twice. Gradually lower knees and return to a march. Finish by walking on the spot for 16 counts.

BODYWISE STRENGTH AND TONE

1 Outer thigh

Lie on one side with back stretched out. Bend lower leg to a 90-
degree angle and straighten upper leg (toes to front) holding it
parallel to the floor. Pull abdominals in and top hip forward.
Lower the upper leg to the floor and then lift it up to hip level.
Do 20–30 slow lifts, then roll over and repeat with other leg.

2   Inner thigh

Lie on one side with both knees bent. Slowly straighten lower leg in line with upper body (the bent leg remains relaxed and bent forward). Lift lower leg (toes pulled towards head) up towards upper leg, tightening inner thigh, then slowly lower. Keep stomach pulled in and back straight. Repeat 10–20 times, then roll over and repeat with other leg.

3   Triceps dips

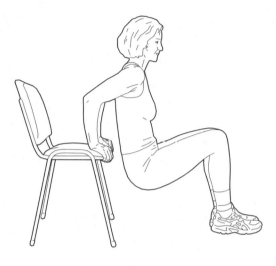

Sit on step or firm chair with knees bent and feet flat to floor. Hold on to edge with hands, keeping them close to your body. Pull stomach in and move bottom forward off step or chair, with arms supporting body weight. Now bend elbows to a 90-degree angle and lower the body for 2 counts, then straighten arms and lift the body up for 2 counts. Do not lock elbows; keep them very slightly bent. Repeat 4 times, then lower and raise for single counts 4–8 times.

4   Triceps stretch

Sit astride a firm chair, with abdominals pulled in and feet flat on floor. Lift arms above head, bend right elbow (right hand towards upper back) and with left hand grip right arm between elbow and shoulder. Gently press head back against right arm until stretch is felt. Hold for 8 counts. Repeat with other arm.

5   Wall press-ups

Stand tall about 3 feet away from a wall, with feet shoulder-width apart and abdominals pulled in. Lean forward with a straight back, placing hands on wall, level with shoulders and shoulder-width apart. Bend arms and lean towards wall for 2 counts, then push away from wall and straighten arms for 2 counts. Repeat 6 times. Then bend and straighten arms for single counts 15–20 times. Keep elbows pointing down to floor and close to body for best effect.

6 Chest and biceps stretch

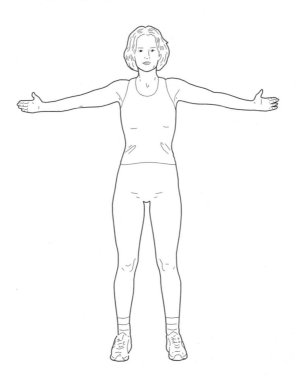

Stand tall with feet hip-width apart, knees slightly bent, bottom tucked under and abdominals pulled in. Relax shoulders down, lengthen arms out wide to your sides and gently press chest forwards. Hold for 6 counts. Release and repeat.

7   Abdominal curl

Lie down with knees bent and feet flat to floor. Place hands behind head with elbows out wide to support the weight of the head. Tilt pelvis upwards and press lower back into floor and pull the abdominals in. Slowly lift chest towards ceiling, flattening the stomach and pulling abdominals in tighter, then lower. Repeat 10–20 times. Keep head back and chin towards ceiling. Exhale on the effort as you lift; inhale as you lower. Keep back pressed to floor.

8   Abdominal oblique

Lie down and lift chest as before, but keep one elbow on floor
and rotate ribs slightly (left shoulder towards right knee). Lift
for 2 counts, lower for 2 counts, repeating 6–10 times. Both
elbows should remain wide. Turn from the waist, not from the
neck. Repeat on other side.

9 Knee hug

Lie down as before with knees bent. Relax back and shoulders into floor. Slowly bring knees towards chest, holding the backs of your thighs. Hold for 10–20 counts. This will stretch lower back and release tension in abdominal area.

10   Knee circles

From above position, keep knees together and slowly circle them in one direction for 4 counts. Repeat in other direction for 4 counts. Make circles as big as you can, massaging as much of the back into the floor as possible.

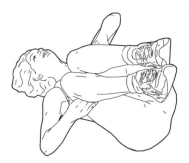

11 Back, outer thigh and neck release

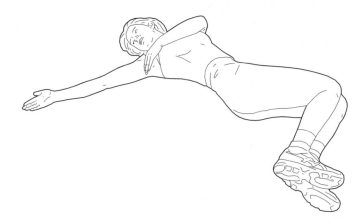

Lie down as before with knees bent. Point toes, keeping them on the floor. Gently drop both knees towards the floor to the left, bringing both arms across the chest to the right side. Look towards your hands and relax; hold for 10 counts. Repeat on other side.

12 Abdominal and full body stretch

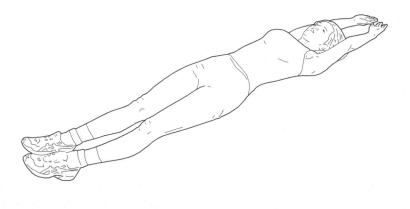

Lie down, raise arms above head and lengthen legs. Feel stretch in abdominals. Now point toes outwards, stretching through the whole body. The lower back may arch slightly, giving a gentle stretch here too. Hold for 8 counts. Relax and repeat 3 times.

13   Deep relaxation

From previous position, slowly bring arms down to sides, palms towards the ceiling. Turn head slightly to one side. Relax legs and allow feet and knees to roll outwards. Take deep breaths and let the body become heavy and sink into the floor. Relax and stay in this position as long as you like!

STEP
FIVE

Stresswise

'There is a pleasure in the pathless woods,
There is a rapture on the lonely shore,
There is society where none intrudes,
By the deep Sea, and Music in its roar.'

LORD BYRON

Stress is inescapable. Reaching into the workplace, our social and home lives, and even intruding on our sleep, stress takes its daily toll on our minds and bodies. Imagine for a moment what you feel like when you are stressed: your mind is wound up, your muscles feel tight, your neck and back are stiff, you're anxious, maybe even depressed. All this adds up to a powerful cocktail, leaving you lacking energy and zest for life.

All kinds of situations can trigger stress-related symptoms, and it's important to recognise your own personal stressors so you can learn how to cope with them. However, one of the main stressors affecting us all is inactivity. Quite simply, we are less physically active than we used to be. Our lifestyles have become increasingly complex and sophisticated, yet our bodies have not evolved to cope with the stresses and strains to which we subject ourselves day in and day out.

Most working environments used to be physically demanding, but the growth of technology has meant that many of us now spend our day in a sedentary posture – in office chairs, cars, buses, trains, taxis and aeroplanes. To make matters worse, at the end of the working day, we drag our sedentary, overstimulated, overstressed bodies back home and spend another two or three hours sitting watching television. And it's as well to remember that an inactive lifestyle slows down our metabolism, so our bodies burn less calories and we put on weight – and this makes us feel even worse!

But the vicious circle doesn't end there. Several studies have shown that the least active among us is twice as likely to have a heart attack as the most active. And an inactive lifestyle is now considered so damaging that both the British Heart Foundation and the American Heart Association list it as a major risk factor on a par with high blood cholesterol, high blood pressure and cigarette smoking.

It makes you stressed just thinking about it! But we can do something about it. We can become aware of the problem and take steps to break through the barrier of tension, stress and inactivity.

STEP AWAY FROM STRESS

'Your steps are the most important thing . . . they decide everything'

THICH NHAT HANH

The easiest, quickest and most effective way to subdue stress is to walk. Walking provides an instant pick-me-up, recharging your batteries after tension and stress have drained them of energy. It is cheap, it can be done anywhere at any time, and its benefits are not only physical, but also psychological. A brisk walk refreshes your body and mind and is the best antidote to tension.

Enthusiasts often talk about the feel-good benefits of a good walk. A brisk walk decreases the stress hormones (epinephrine and norepinephrine) and increases the relaxation hormones in the brain (endorphins), those mood-elevating hormones which energise you and make you feel on top of the world. Movement makes you feel alive.

The human body is not built for sitting still: it is designed to move. When we sit, the force of gravity tends to pull our head and shoulders forward, placing undue strain on the neck muscles and spine. Sitting hunched in this position for much of the day, the cumulative strain can eventually translate into physical trauma such as neck ache, backache, headaches, and other tension-related problems such as high blood pressure and insomnia. Simply adopting a relaxed walking posture (walking tall, head level, shoulders and arms relaxed, with freely swinging hips) distances the body from the tension danger points of a sitting position.

WHAT THE EXPERTS SAY ABOUT WALKING

Taking a brisk walk can be as good as, and probably even better than, having a rest. Dr Hans Selye, author of *The Stress of Life*, said 'voluntary change of activity is as good as a rest'. The Rockport Walking Institute in the United States advises:

> Walking is a healthy, natural function of the human body. Because of the structure, shape and flexibility of the spine, the body is better suited for walking than for sitting, standing or running. Walking is . . . like a perfect massage; it will ease and relax the muscles . . . reducing stress.

And the writer Robert Louis Stevenson, another great walker, had this to say about the anti-stress benefits of walking, in an age which was much less frenetic than our own: 'To all who feel overwhelmed and work weary, the exhilarating exercise of walking offers both a stimulus and a sedative.' So if you feel tense or anxious, get outside in the open air and walk your tensions away. The increased flow of oxygen through the body and the natural rhythmical action of walking – the pendulum motion of the arms and legs: one, two; one, two – drain away muscle tension, leaving you feeling pleasantly relaxed.

As you walk, the feet carry the whole weight of the body, holding it upright and maintaining the body's balance. Balance begins with the feet, and a balanced body moving through space develops a sense of harmony that leads to a balanced mind. It is the orchestration of balance and grace of movement that makes walking the best exercise to combat tension and stress.

AWAKENING THE SPINE

You are walking along the street, lost in your own thoughts, when suddenly you catch a glimpse of yourself in a shop window. 'Is that really me?' you gasp in horror, as you stare at the hunched, round-shouldered slouch reflected back at you. Then your thoughts rewind to all those times when your mother nagged you to sit or stand up straight. And then you realise why correct posture is so important.

Poor posture is caused mainly by a lack of muscle strength, particularly in the upper body. Sitting in one place for much of the working day, carrying heavy loads and frequent bending all put prolonged strain on the spine. And being overweight or pregnant stresses the spine. But relax: there's always time to straighten up and awaken the spine.

We've already looked at the importance of our posture when we walk, but it's just as important to give some thought to our posture during the working day when we are liable to slouch at a desk. F. Matthias Alexander, who perfected the Alexander Technique, suggests the following posture check when walking, standing and sitting:

- Let the neck be relaxed and free to avoid increasing muscle tension in the neck.
- Let the head go forward and up, never back and down to sit on and crush the spine.
- Let the torso lengthen and widen out to avoid arching the spine.

When standing, sitting, or walking, breathe deeply from the abdomen and try to imagine an invisible thread running up through your body from feet to crown, pulling you upwards. With practice, you will find your body settling into a natural, graceful posture which will get you through the day without undue strain.

Good posture is more than just correct body alignment. It has important psychological benefits, boosting your self-esteem and giving others the impression that you are alert and confident. It's a sure-fire way to keep stress at bay.

It's as well to remember that, even with the best posture, sitting still for too long will place unnecessary stress on the spine, neck and shoulders. The best advice is to take regular breaks, get up and walk around, and take the time to do a few stretches. The following stretches can be performed at your desk. They will help keep your body relaxed and supple amid the troubles and tensions of the working day.

1 Shoulder shrugs/rolls

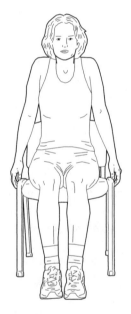

With arms relaxed, slowly lift shoulders upwards to ears, then lower. Repeat 4 times. Now press shoulders forward, separating shoulder blades, then squeeze backwards, shoulder blades together. Repeat 4 times. Repeat shrugs and rolls twice.

2   Upper back stretch

Sit tall, grab one hand on top of other and press palms forward
(arms extended in front). Separate shoulder blades, stretching
across upper back. Relax chin down to chest to gently lengthen
and relax back of neck. Hold for 4 counts.

3   Upper back and torso stretch

Looking straight ahead, take palms up towards ceiling and reach up to stretch upper back and waist. Hold for 8–10 counts.

4 Chest stretch

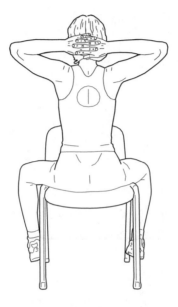

Sitting tall, interlace fingers, take palms behind head (hands about half an inch away from head). Open elbows out wide, squeeze shoulder blades together and feel stretch across the chest. Hold for 8 counts. Relax.

5   Back stretch

Sit back into chair, feet parallel a little wider than shoulder-width apart. Slowly lower body forward, resting chest on thighs, allowing the head, neck and arms to hang relaxed towards the floor. Hold for 6–8 counts. Slowly roll up through the spine, lifting head and shoulders last, back to your sitting position.

6 Ankle stretch

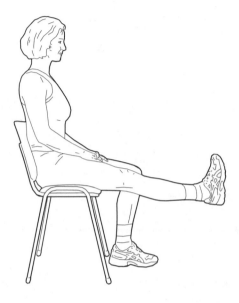

Sitting on a chair, lift one foot off floor, point toes forward and hold the stretch across top of foot for 4 counts. Now flex foot backwards, pulling toes back towards body, and hold for 4 counts, feeling stretch behind lower leg. Slowly rotate foot, drawing a large circle one way, then the other, 4–6 times. Repeat with other foot.

7   Squats

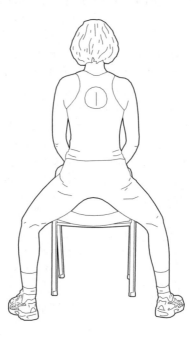

Holding on to back of chair for balance, turn toes outwards and stand tall, lifting through top of head. Tighten buttocks and lengthen leg muscles. Now slowly bend knees into a squatting position (keeping hips just above knee level). Hold for 5 counts, slowly stand up and repeat. Feel stretch in hips, groin and inner thighs. Repeat 4 times.

EVERY BREATH YOU TAKE

'One must breathe the essence of life, regulate one's respiration
to preserve one's spirit and keep the muscles relaxed.'

HUANG DI (2698–2589 BC)

In China it's known as *chi* or *qi*, in Japan, *ki*, and in India, *prana*.
It is the body's flow of natural energy that lies dormant inside
until we release it by stimulating the breath. Stress can take its
toll on our breathing. When we are stressed, we tend to breathe
from the upper part of the chest only and our breathing is more
rapid and shallow. This means that the oxygen level of our blood
drops and the carbon-dioxide level is hiked up, and we have to
breathe harder. In contrast, deep breathing from the abdomen,
using our full lung capacity, has an energising, revitalising effect.

Breathing from the chest alone puts increased strain on the
heart, which has to pump more blood to carry the same amount
of oxygen, whereas efficient abdominal breathing gives your
body an 'oxygen bath', pumping a rich supply to the lungs,
blood and cells. And the benefits extend beyond the physical. By
stimulating your breath, you will become calmer, more relaxed
and focused.

We can now begin to see how posture (whether walking,
standing or sitting) and the way we breathe are connected, and
why it is so important to breathe correctly. By taking slow, natural, deep breaths, you can more than double the volume of air
you inhale with each breath. Sit comfortably with your spine
straight. Relax your shoulders, your abdomen, your eye muscles,
and your lower jaw, and bring your awareness to your breathing.
Then practise the following technique:

1. Inhale slowly, allowing the breath to enter effortlessly through
   the nose. At the same time, push out your abdomen as though
   it were a balloon expanding.
2. When your abdomen is stretched, expand your chest with
   air, to fill the middle part of your lungs.

3. If you now allow your abdomen to pull in slightly, you will feel your shoulders and collar bones begin to rise, filling your upper lungs with air.
4. Slowly begin to exhale through the nose, allowing your abdomen to contract. This will lift the diaphragm and release the air in your lungs, opening up space for fresh air to enter.

Aim to make your exhalation longer than your inhalation and don't hold your breath in between. To begin with, practise for five minutes. Then, as you become comfortable with the technique, gradually increase to ten and then 15 minutes. If at any time you feel dizzy, stop. By ensuring that your exhalations are complete, you will expel more carbon dioxide and more of the cells' waste products, and gain more from each breath of fresh air. One way to check if you are breathing correctly is to put your hands on your abdomen. It should swell when you breathe in and sink when you breathe out. Lying on your back in the deep-relaxation position (see page 142) is a good way to practise this.

You can use deep abdominal breathing at any time as a rapid stressbuster. Whenever you feel tense and anxious, bring your awareness into the moment; then centre yourself and take a quick breather. By focusing on your breath for a few minutes, you will find yourself becoming calmer and more relaxed.

Of course, brisk walking is an excellent way to develop abdominal breathing. Being an aerobic exercise, brisk walking uses the full capacity of the lungs. And it makes them more efficient by opening more useable lung space for taking in oxygen from the atmosphere with every breath you take.

PEACE OF MIND AT EVERY STEP

'I walked in the woods
All by myself,
To seek nothing
That was on my mind.'

GOETHE

Like breathing, the simple act of walking is often carried out
with little awareness. You only have to look around to see the
way many people are slaves to their bodies – shuffling along the
pavement, heads craning forwards, pulled along by their necks.
In contrast, a confident person walks tall in a relaxed, alert posture, their eyes looking straight ahead, maintaining a concentrated
awareness.

Although you can increase the effectiveness of walking by
paying attention to your posture in this way, it's also possible to
add a further dimension to your routine by making your walk
the focus of meditation. Walking meditation is a way to connect
with your deepest reality. It is a way to still the mind, to relax, to
let go and surrender to your own natural rhythms.

You can walk slowly or quickly, indoors or out; walk along a
beach, in a park, or in your garden; wear shoes or go barefoot.
But remember to begin by centring yourself in the relaxed, aware
posture we have discussed. Correct alignment of the body is
important: it allows your energy to flow through to your arms
and legs. Try the following meditations. The first concentrates
on your body movement and the rhythm of walking; the second
is a meditation focusing on the elements of breathing, counting
and stepping.

Calm awareness

Walking mindfully, bring your awareness to your movement through the air: the spring of your heels and toes as they propel you forward; the pull of your muscles in your feet, legs and hips, and the to-and-fro rhythm of your arms and legs. Try to visualise the tension and tightness of your muscles melting away and dissolving as you walk. Stay centred with these feelings and explore them. Allow yourself to merge into the rhythm and beauty of the moment and feel the flow of energy through your body. If thoughts intrude into your mind, acknowledge their presence, then let them pass away, like bubbles rising and dispersing. By walking in this calm, focused way, you will be bringing into balance your inner and outer worlds – body and spirit.

Breathing easy

Walking more slowly than usual, focus on the cycle of your breath, and allow it to find its own natural rhythm. In order to concentrate on breathing and walking at the same time, you need to identify your breathing with your steps, by counting the steps. Do this by measuring the length of your breath by the number of steps you take during that breath. Count how many steps you take when you breathe out and how many steps you take when you breathe in. Don't try to control your breathing to fit in with your steps. If you find that your breath only lasts for, say, two-and-a-half steps, then speed up a little so that your three steps fit into one breath. Your exhalation may be longer than your inhalation, perhaps four steps. That's fine. Experiment a little to find a rhythm you feel comfortable with. By counting breaths in this way, we are making contact with the basic rhythm of the universe: the inhaling and exhaling of our lungs is like the ebb and flow of the oceans and the movement of the planets.

AT THE END OF THE DAY: PROGRESSIVE RELAXATION

Progressive relaxation is a method developed by an American doctor, Edmund Jacobson, in about 1910. It involves recognising tension and then letting go of it step by step, by progressively contracting and relaxing each of the body muscles. You simply ask your neck to relax . . . and it relaxes; ask your shoulder to relax . . . and it relaxes; ask your leg to relax . . . and it relaxes. It's the perfect way at the end of the day to drain away residual stress that may prevent you winding down.

Find a quiet place where you will not be interrupted and lie down in the deep-relaxation position as shown on page 142 (or, if you prefer, sit in a comfortable chair). Then close your eyes and breathe normally.

- Begin relaxing your body by bringing awareness to your toes. Contract the muscles in the big toe of your right foot and hold for 5 seconds. Release and feel all the tension draining away. As your awareness moves through the body, name each part of the body silently while visualising it in your mind and contract then relax, like this: big toe . . . second toe . . . third toe . . . fourth toe . . . fifth toe.
- Now shift your awareness up through your right foot to your ankle, and continue the process: heel . . . sole . . . ball of right foot . . . ankle.
- Now shift your awareness to your left foot and repeat the process, moving from big toe up to ankle. Continue repeating the method, moving up to lower legs (front), lower legs (rear), knees, thighs, hips, buttocks, abdomen, lower back, upper back, chest, hands, arms, shoulders, neck, back of head, top of head, forehead, jaw and facial muscles.

When you have finished this sequence, maintain awareness of your breathing for a few moments and bask awhile in this state of complete relaxation.

Feet First

How to keep your feet and legs healthy

'Wings for the angels, but feet for men'

Josiah Gilbert Holland

'The true man breathes with his heels'

Chuang-tzu

Most feet begin life as perfectly shaped structures, but by middle age their owners will have turned them into distorted and poorly functioning objects. Our feet, which take the brunt of all our weight-bearing activity, were designed to walk on soft, natural surfaces like soil and sand. But each day we subject them to a pounding of 2000 tons by walking on hard, unnatural surfaces like pavements and floors. And we compound the problem by cramming our feet into ill-fitting, airless footwear for most of the year, subjecting them to ailments, deformities and infections. Yet with just a little care and attention, plus some common sense, we can have trouble-free feet.

Footnotes

Compared to the number of bones between your hip and ankle – a mere four, including the kneecap – there are 26 bones in each foot.

The poet, William Wordsworth, is said to have walked 186,000 miles during his lifetime.

THE RIGHT SHOES

'I measure your health by the number of shoes you have worn out'

RALPH WALDO EMERSON

Throughout this book we've suggested that one of the reasons walking is such a great form of exercise is because it's inexpensive – the only equipment you need is a pair of comfortable, supportive, 'walkable' shoes. Well-designed walking shoes act like shock absorbers. They take the strain out of walking; they keep your feet in good shape; and they will help keep the rest of you in good shape, too.

Although walking is a low-impact, low-stress exercise (walking places a force of only one to one-and-a-half times body weight on the joints, compared with three to four times body weight for high-impact sports like running and aerobics), it is still necessary to look after your feet. And the easiest way to do that is to give some thought to the type of shoes you wear. What makes a good 'walkable' shoe? Following the tips overleaf will help you choose the right shoe.

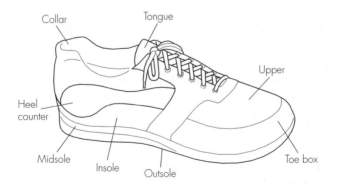

Heel counter. The heel counter wraps around the heel and helps to control excess pronation (see Foot Facts, overleaf) and rear-foot wobble. A good heel counter provides stability for the entire foot and leg. It should be firm, cushioned and reinforced, but not over-padded.

Collar. Look for a padded heel collar with a notch or a dip in the back of the collar. This cradles the Achilles tendon and reduces the pressure on it.

Insole. The part of the shoe your foot rests on. It should be lined, cushioned and removable, and should be made from a material that absorbs perspiration.

Outsole. This is the bottom of the shoe that comes into contact with the ground. It should provide durability, and should be shock-absorbent to protect your feet from bruising. It should be almost flat, with little or no heel, and the tread should be patterned for good traction.

Tongue. The tongue should be padded to protect the top of the foot.

Midsole. The midsole's key role is shock absorption, providing cushioning and firmness for support. It should flex at the ball of the foot but be hard to bend at the arch and heel.

Upper. This should be sturdy, providing good support, and made from a breathable fabric, either canvas, leather, or a composite material such as leather-nylon mesh. Check inside for raised seams that could rub and cause blisters.

Toe box. Your toes should be able to move easily up and down and back and forth. There should be a space the width of your thumbnail between the end of the toe box and the tip of the longest toe on your longer foot.

FOOT FACTS

If you take a close look at a pair of worn shoes, you will notice there is excessive wear to one side of the heel. Biomechanical studies have shown that most walkers land on the outside of their heels; they then rotate their weight on to the inside of their heels before rolling their weight forward on to the ball of the foot, a tendency known as pronation. Pronation works like a braking mechanism, but too much of it can create a twisting motion, which can cause ankle, knee and hip injuries. To make matters worse, there is a tendency for the rear foot to wobble when you walk. You can see now why it is necessary to wear a shoe that gives you the right support and cushioning.

When you shop for a new shoe, do it later in the day, since your feet tend to swell slightly as the day wears on. Wear socks like the ones you will be walking in and try both shoes on to test for comfort and fit. Stand up and walk around the shop before making a final decision to buy.

PAMPERING YOUR FEET

You may think that your feet are tough, but walking on surfaces as different as concrete, earth and sand can take their toll. A comfortable walking shoe is one way to deal with the problem; another way is to pamper your feet a little with good-quality walking socks. Feet can sweat as much as a cup of perspiration a day and moisture is the main culprit in causing blisters. Walking socks not only protect the feet from injury, they also disperse or 'wick away' perspiration which would otherwise damage the lining of your shoes.

The fit of your walking sock is as important as the fit of your shoe. The best socks are padded and cushioned and draw perspiration away from your feet, leaving them cool and dry.

Natural fibres like cotton absorb moisture, whereas the best walking socks tend to be either a cotton/synthetic blend or entirely synthetic, both of which allow moisture to evaporate. Look for socks with generous padding on the heel and the ball of the foot. You really will be walking on air.

Should you wear one pair of socks or two? In cold weather, two pairs help to keep out the cold, but as a general rule, it's best to experiment and find your own comfort level. Some people suggest wearing a thin inner pair of cotton socks to prevent chafing and a thicker outer pair to cushion the feet and keep them warm and absorb sweat. It is a question of trial and error. You will probably find that one pair of good-quality cushioned socks will be more than satisfactory.

A final tip: fungus thrives in a warm, sweaty environment, and if you are not careful, it can cause infection. Change your socks every day, and carry a spare pair on long walks if your feet perspire a lot. If you keep your feet sweet and pamper them a little, they will reward you with endless miles of trouble-free walking.

FOOT FAULTS AND THEIR REMEDIES

I can hear you saying now: 'I thought you said that walking is one of the safest forms of exercise, so why should I get injured or suffer problems with my feet?'

You're quite right. But then walking itself does not cause injuries or foot ailments. Complaints such as blisters, shin pain, corns and callouses, and athlete's foot are often caused by

- poorly fitting shoes
- poor-quality, badly fitting socks
- inadequate warm-up
- problems with road surface
- overtraining
- poor walking technique
- a combination of all these factors

Although basic hygiene such as washing and regular nail-cutting may be all that is required to keep your feet in good health, when normal feet turn into problem feet, it's important to take action so that short-term pain doesn't turn into long-term damage. Here are some of the most common foot faults.

Athlete's foot

This common fungal infection thrives in warm, damp environ-ments (sweaty socks are ideal!), and usually occurs between the toes, particularly the outer toes, but it can also affect the toe-nails. There may be red scaling and tiny blisters and the affected area may become itchy. You can prevent fungal infection by washing your feet at least once a day with soap and tepid water, then drying gently but thoroughly between the toes.

Footwear creates the conditions necessary for warmth and moisture, so take preventative action by keeping your feet clean and dry. Wear well-fitting shoes made of materials that breathe, such as leather or canvas, and socks that disperse moisture. Change socks or stockings at least once a day and alternate your shoes so that they have a chance to air between wearings. It takes at least 24 hours for a pair of shoes to air and dry out thoroughly.

If you have a fungal infection, there are several over-the-counter creams and powders available, but toenail infections are more difficult to treat and you may need to pay a visit to the chiropodist.

Blisters

Blisters are caused by continuous friction against the skin due to badly fitting shoes or socks. Formed by the layers of skin cells separating and filling with fluid, blisters often form during hot weather, when the feet sweat and swell, or if shoes and sandals are worn without socks or stockings.

Small blisters can be left to heal naturally, after first cleaning them and covering with a sterile dressing. If a blister is very large, you may want to puncture it first. To do this, sterilise a needle with antiseptic and prick the edge of the blister. Then blot up the liquid, clean the area with antiseptic and cover with a sterile gauze pad.

The best treatment for blisters is prevention. With good hygiene, proper exercise and appropriate footwear, your feet should never have a chance to develop blisters.

Bunions

Bunions are a condition in which the side of the big-toe joint (the metatarso-phalangeal joint) becomes enlarged and painful. The tendency to develop bunions may be hereditary, and flat-footed people are more likely to get them. In women, bunions can be caused by wearing high-heeled shoes with pointed toes. Sufferers should wear comfortable shoes that avoid pressing on the affected bone.

The deformity of the toe bone, usually of the second, third or fourth toes, known as hammer-toes, is more common in women and is again caused by high-heeled shoes with pointed toes. Corrective pads can help, but the best treatment is to wear well-fitting, comfortable shoes.

If you think you are developing a bunion, switch to shoes with a low heel and ample toe box. And avoid any shoes or stockings with seams that put pressure on the big-toe joint. If the deformity is painful or hinders walking, seek professional advice.

Corns and callouses

Corns and callouses are the result of pressure and chafing on cramped toes. Hard corns develop on top of toes, soft corns between toes. With corns, the skin thickens and a core of dead skin develops. Callouses are areas of hard skin, affecting either the toes, the ball of the foot or the heel. Both conditions can be prevented by wearing comfortable shoes that fit properly.

Corns and callouses can be treated by soaking the foot in warm water every day and gently rubbing the built-up skin with a pumice stone or foot file – the surface will gradually peel away. You may have to follow this procedure a few times; be careful not to rub too hard as it will make the skin raw. Afterwards, protect the tender area with a lambswool or moleskin pad or a bandage.

Ingrowing toenails

An ingrowing toenail usually develops when the side of a big toenail cuts into the soft toe tissue, causing redness and swelling and sometimes infection. The most common cause is cutting toenails incorrectly. Tight, uncomfortable shoes and hosiery can make matters worse.

There are several things you can do to prevent ingrowing toenails: keep your feet clean with regular bathing; dry them thoroughly and apply a foot powder; wear comfortable shoes that allow the feet to breathe; and wear clean socks each day, choosing ones that wick away moisture. Always use proper nail-clippers and cut the nails straight across, following the shape of the toe.

If you have an ingrowing toenail, first try to determine and eliminate the cause – perhaps tight shoes or stockings pressing the nail into the tissue of the big toe. Then soak the toe in warm water to soften the nail and put some strands of absorbent cotton under the toenail to prevent the nail from digging into the skin. If there is swelling or if the condition is very painful, a doctor or chiropodist can cut away the ingrown toenail and treat the infection with antibiotics.

Walker's heel

The heel is put under a great deal of stress during walking, and there is a thick layer of fatty tissue under the heel which acts as a shock absorber. As you grow older, these shock-absorbing pads get thinner and repeated pressure on the bone and muscle in the heel can bring on painful heel syndrome, or walker's heel. It is particularly severe when you swing your weight on to your feet first thing in the morning, or when you get up after a long period of sitting. Being overweight can add to the problem, as can prolonged periods of standing. Inflammation of the joints, nerves and tendons can also cause heel pain. These conditions – arthritis, neuritis and tendinitis – require medical treatment.

The best treatment for walker's heel may be to rest, taking the pressure off your heel, and to limit your exercise to non-weight-bearing activities such as swimming and cycling. Shoes are also important. Ensure they are comfortable with thickly cushioned heels. If necessary, insert a shock-absorbing heel pad. If severe pain strikes, take an over-the-counter painkiller and apply an ice pack for 15 minutes or so. Ultrasound pain therapy and surgery are sometimes needed, but in most cases the problem should clear up fairly quickly.

One cause of pain is plantar fasciitis, an inflammation of the plantar fascia – the tough fibrous band that connects the heel bone to the front of the foot. An insole in your walking shoe will provide some cushioning and comfort to the heel and redirect pressure away from the painful spot.

Achilles tendinitis

The Achilles tendon may become painful at the back of the heel, near where it attaches to the heel bone, both during and after exercise. Walkers don't normally suffer from a complete or partial rupture of the tendon, but the inflammation may be bad enough to produce a visible swelling at the back of the heel and discomfort when walking. The condition can be caused by inadequate walking shoes or by a sudden change of routine, such as wearing a different type of shoe or walking on a different surface.

To prevent the condition, build up your walking programme gradually, making sure that you warm up by walking slowly before you start to stride out briskly. And always perform your post-walk stretches, particularly the stretches to loosen the calf muscles.

If you injure your Achilles tendon, avoid overstretching and walk at a moderate pace and only on flat surfaces. Rest and applying ice packs or cold compresses will help; you should also make sure that your shoes give you the correct support.

How to keep your legs healthy

Shin splints

Walkers suffer very few injuries due to their chosen form of exercise, but one problem that does sometimes crop up is shin soreness. A shin splint is characterised by tenderness and burning in the shin, occurring when the muscles attached to your shin have pulled away from the bone. A catch-all term, 'shin splint' refers to a family of overuse injuries causing inflammation of the muscles and tendons in the lower leg. A common cause is pounding the feet on hard surfaces. Shin splints can be particularly painful in walkers who go up and down hills. In novice walkers, the condition emerges as a result of asking the muscles in the front of your shin to do more than they are prepared to do.

You can treat shin splints by cutting back on your normal walking routine or, in cases of severe pain, by taking a few days off. And if necessary, apply ice and elevate the legs.

To lessen the risk of shin splints, wear well-cushioned shoes with good support. Avoid hard surfaces, and don't suddenly increase the intensity of your workout. And begin a regular routine of stretching and strengthening the front leg muscles. The following exercises will help you to warm up and prepare the necessary muscles prior to walking.

Ankle circles

Stand on one foot and make large circles in the air with the toes of your raised foot (you may need to hold on to something for balance). The leg should be held steady so that the circle is made by rolling the ankle. Do five to ten circles in each direction, then repeat with the other foot.

Toe points

Lift the foot, point the toe, feeling the stretch through the ankle, and hold for a count of ten. Repeat with the other foot. These also make an easy stretch after a walk, and you can do them anywhere, even while sitting.

Strains and sprains

These are the most common type of injury, usually resulting from a single incident, involving sharp pain, and often accompanied by swelling. They are especially common among over-eager walkers who try to push too hard, too soon, and who neglect to warm up and cool down correctly.

A strain or 'muscle pull' is the stretching or tearing of a muscle or tendon, and for walkers the most common sites for strains are the hamstring and quadriceps muscles. The best way to prevent strains is to warm up these large muscle groups so as to increase blood flow and raise their temperature. You can keep these muscles flexible by performing the post-walk stretches at the end of each walk.

A sprain is the stretching or tearing of a ligament – the bands connecting bones together. Sprains tend to be more serious than strains, partly because they take longer to heal, but also because a torn ligament can throw bones out of alignment, causing damage to other tissues, and therefore sprains may require medical attention. Strong, flexible muscles help protect against sprains, so strengthen and stretch the hamstrings and quadriceps regularly using the post-walk stretches.

These muscle-overuse injuries can be relieved with the RICE principle: *Rest* the joint; apply *Ice* to reduce inflammation; apply *Compression* or wrap in an elastic bandage (not too tight), also to reduce inflammation; and *Elevate* the injury above heart level. Swelling of the joint should be reduced in 24 to 48 hours. But be careful not to risk another injury by exercising again too soon.

Muscle cramps

Although muscle cramps are harmless and do not involve actual injury, when they happen they can be quite painful. They can occur in any muscle at any time, but they most often occur in the calf or foot. A muscle contraction or spasm, causing cramp, can happen during activity or when resting. When exercising, causes include coldness and tiredness, excessive sweating, dehydration, and unconditioned muscles being fatigued or over-stretched. Stretching your calf muscles can help (see exercises on pages 26 and 29), as can drinking plenty of water before and during exercise, especially in hot weather.

You can also find relief from cramp by massaging the muscles or applying an ice pack to the area, helping to relax it. Walking may help, particularly if you put your full weight on your heels.

The two best ways to avoid foot problems and to help your legs to shape up are to walk regularly and follow a daily routine of basic foot hygiene. If you also wear comfortable and supportive shoes, warm up and cool down before and after each walk, and exercise to strengthen and stretch muscles, you should enjoy many miles of injury-free walking.

STEP
SEVEN

Walk For Life

Maintaining a healthy lifestyle

You don't need to spend hours in the gym to get fit. You just need to use your body in the way nature designed it to be used. Human beings are not meant to spend hours every day hunched over office desks, cramped behind the wheel of a car or slumped in front of the television. They are meant to move around and be active. And the easiest way to be active and stay active is to walk regularly.

By following the 30-Day Walking Workout you will have made a good start. But that's not enough. You have to be able to stick with it for the rest of your life – even if you've never been able to before. Studies show that most of the fitness gains made will be lost in a few months if you cease to exercise. And changes made to improve your diet will vanish if you don't consciously build new eating patterns into your everyday lifestyle.

In this chapter, we will show you how to keep up a fitness and healthy-eating routine; how to fire your enthusiasm with commitment; and how to build consistent, long-term habits that will serve you for the rest of your life.

KEEPING IT UP

'If one just keeps on walking everything will be all right'
SØREN KIERKEGAARD

Maintaining a healthy lifestyle is all about regular habits – building a long-term routine that is enjoyable and fun to do. By beginning with small habits, such as taking a walking break instead of a coffee break, and gradually cutting down on fat and processed foods, you will be able to build long-term habits that will become as automatic as cleaning your teeth or having a shower.

To kick-start your maintenance routine, we have put together a summary of some of the principles for exercise and healthy eating that we have discussed throughout the book, along with some suggestions for how to put them all into practice.

WAKING UP

Deep breathing

Once you are roused from sleep, lie on your back and start the day with two or three minutes of deep abdominal breathing to get your circulation going and give yourself an oxygen boost. It really will give you that get-up-and-go feeling.

Think positive thoughts

Don't let your mind wander back to any thoughts that were worrying you the night before. Centre yourself in the present moment and tell yourself that today is a new day bringing new challenges and new opportunities. Make a few mental plans of when and where you are going to walk today. Then get out of bed.

Drink water

The best drink of the day. Your body needs water – lots of it. Begin the day with a glass or two to rehydrate all your biological functions. Water is an instant pick-me-up, so drink plenty throughout the day whenever you are thirsty or feel drained. Remember that drinks containing caffeine or alcohol actually dehydrate the body, so you lose fluid rather than gaining it.

Eat a healthy breakfast

Start the day with a nutritious breakfast. Studies show that people who eat a healthy breakfast have more energy and perform better at work. Don't be tempted to skip breakfast and manage on just a cup of coffee. By mid-morning you will be hungry and in danger of reaching for a snack which may not have any real nutritional value. Better to take your choice from The Walker's Diet Breakfasts in the 30-Day Healthy-Eating Plan and give yourself a head start to the day.

Start a walking and healthy-eating diary

Keep a record of your commitment and consistency by writing your goals down on paper. Simply writing down each day's planned walks and your ideas for healthy eating (snacks, food purchases, meals) will help you to keep track of your progress and stay motivated.

Fit in a morning walk

Don't be put off by lack of time – if necessary, get up ten minutes earlier. It will do you far more good than the extra sleep. Dress in comfortable clothes and supportive shoes and head out of the door. Walk for five minutes, then turn around and walk back. Your muscles may be a little stiff when you first wake up, so, to get your circulation going and avoid injury, remember to warm up by walking slowly for a few minutes. Cool down in the same way, and finish with three quick stretches – calf, hamstring and quadriceps.

Another option is to consider walking to work, if it's within easy distance, or perhaps leaving your car further away from the office than usual and walking the rest of the way.

TRAVELLING TO WORK

Good posture

Since you are likely to spend a large part of your day sitting down, begin the day by making sure your posture is well aligned. Whether in the car, bus or train on the way to work, try to keep your spine erect and shoulders relaxed. And breathe deeply from the abdomen to set a healthy rhythm for the day. As your day progresses, take regular posture checks whenever you feel yourself slouching. You will have far more energy and will be less likely to suffer from tension and stress.

Collect your thoughts

If you are on public transport on your way to work, take a few moments to sit quietly, relax your body, and collect your thoughts. Rather than simply being swept along in the whirl of daily activity, just close your eyes for a few minutes and visualise a peaceful, calm place where you would like to be. Then bask in this awareness and let its energy wash through you. Being centred in this way puts you in control of your day.

Get off a stop early

If you are on public transport, to notch up those extra aerobic miles, get off the bus or train one or two stops early and walk the rest of the way. You will arrive at your destination with a clear head and glowing with energy.

NINE TO FIVE

Manage your time

Take some stress out of your day by planning ahead. Make a 'To Do' list of daily tasks in order of priority and tackle the activities in order of decreasing pay-off. Spend a few minutes at the end of the day to review the day and plan for tomorrow.

Eat a healthy lunch

A nutritious lunch will give you the energy you need in the middle of the day. Follow the recipes from The Walker's Diet and add a few little extras to the meal – crudités (raw vegetables cut into bite-size pieces), fresh fruit, dried fruit, a few nuts and/or seeds or some low-fat natural yogurt. Eating carbohydrate- and protein-rich foods at lunchtime will see you through the afternoon and early evening.

Take a walking break

Pre-empt the mid-afternoon slump by taking an energising aerobic walk during your lunch hour. Walk alone, take a colleague, or start your own walking group. During the afternoon, try taking ten-minute walk breaks instead of coffee breaks. Take your lead from Jane Austen, an enthusiastic walker, who had one of her characters say: 'The afternoon was made for walking.'

Stretch regularly

As the day wears on, muscles tend to contract as you sit hunched over a desk or computer screen. The neck and shoulder muscles, in particular, can become tense and stiff and this can trigger a headache. Avoid this syndrome by taking regular stretching breaks. Follow the desk-stretching routine on pages 148–54 at least once a day, and repeat whenever you feel your muscles are tight and wound up.

EVENING

Winding down

The wise philosopher Erasmus said: 'Before supper walk a little; after supper do the same.' A brisk walk, or perhaps a quiet stroll, is a relaxing way to help drain away muscular tension built up during the day. And an evening walk can help you sleep. 'If you can't sleep, try walking,' Charles Dickens said.

The evening meal

Take the time to enjoy a delicious, nutritious meal. A meal is about more than just consuming food; it is something to be enjoyed, whether eating with others or alone. Refer to The Walker's Diet for ideas and recipes. Avoid eating too late and don't be tempted to eat too much – you will feel much better, and it is much healthier.

Getting ready for sleep

Towards the end of the day, a few gentle Bodywise stretches (see pages 132–42) will help disperse excess energy and relax away any muscular aches and pains before you sleep. You began your day by lying in bed breathing deeply. Round off your day now with a few minutes of the same.

WEEKENDS

Get back to nature

What a difference a week makes! Take a look at your walking diary and add together all the miles you have clocked up. Congratulate yourself on your enterprise and allow yourself to bathe in the quiet calm of success. Then, during the weekend, build on your success by introducing new scenery with hill walks, park or trail walks, or walks by the sea. Walking is the mini-vacation that you can take at any time.

Take the talking cure

The weekend is an opportunity to spend quality time with family and friends and 'walk the talk'. Sometimes even the most troublesome problems resolve themselves when shared during a good walk. The swinging, rhythmic action of walking unites the conscious and unconscious mind, and sparks creativity. That's certainly what Charles Darwin suggested when he said: 'I can remember the very spot on the road when to my joy the solution occurred to me.'

Fitness for the spirit

Cultivate a quiet oasis at the end of your week with walking meditation. By centring your awareness on the movement of the body or by counting steps, you will allow your mind to relax and free itself from the clutter of chaotic thoughts. Fitness walking stretches our body; inner walking stretches our mind and spirit. This is the true meaning of recreation: re-creation, putting you back together again and making you whole.

KEEPING UP A HEALTHY-EATING ROUTINE

When you have completed the 30-Day Walker's Diet and you are enjoying your new feelings of energy and vitality, you will want to maintain the lifestyle changes you have recently made. So to continue eating healthily, use the recipes from the 30-Day Healthy-Eating Plan or adapt some of your favourite recipes so that they are high in nutritious ingredients and low in fat. Then, by following the principles of the Healthy-Eating Pyramid (see page 79) and Further Food Facts for Fitness Walkers (see page 191), you can continue to enjoy a balanced diet.

Entertaining friends

When you are entertaining friends, select recipes from the 30-Day Plan and simply multiply the quantities to match the number of friends. If you also wish to prepare a starter for a special meal, many of the Light Meals in the 30-Day Plan can be used as an appetising first course, such as Roast Peppers with Almonds (Day 7) or Mexican Salad (Day 13). Here are some other ideas for first courses, each serving two people.

Smoked Salmon Parcels
2 large slices smoked salmon
100 g (4 oz) cooked peeled prawns
10 ml (2 tsp) low-fat mayonnaise
5 ml (1 tsp) lemon juice
2 lemon wedges
freshly ground black pepper

Lay the slices of smoked salmon on a chopping board. Cut the prawns into small pieces and mix with the mayonnaise and lemon juice. Spoon on to the smoked salmon, then fold the smoked salmon to make a parcel. Arrange parcels on individual plates and add some freshly ground pepper. Garnish with the lemon wedges.

Parma Ham and Asparagus
4 slices Parma ham
8 asparagus spears
50 g (2 oz) Parmesan cheese
freshly ground black pepper

Lightly cook the asparagus in boiling water until tender, then leave to cool. Lay the slices of ham on a chopping board and put two asparagus spears on each slice of ham. Roll the ham loosely around the asparagus and place the rolls on individual plates. Cut the Parmesan cheese into thin shavings with a vegetable peeler and scatter over the Parma ham rolls, then add some freshly ground pepper.

Smoked Trout Pâté
1 fillet smoked trout
75 g (3 oz) low-fat cottage cheese
10 ml (2 tsp) creamed horseradish
10 ml (2 tsp) lemon juice
freshly ground black pepper

Flake the fish. Put the cottage cheese into a bowl and crush it with a fork, making it as smooth as possible. Put the flaked fish, horseradish and lemon juice into the bowl with the cottage cheese and mix thoroughly. Spoon on to individual plates and add some freshly ground pepper. Serve with brown bread.

Avocado and Crab
1 small avocado
1 small dressed crab
2 lemon wedges
freshly ground black pepper

Gently mix together the white and brown crab meat, then arrange each portion in the middle of an individual plate. Cut the avocado in half lengthways and remove the skin from each half and discard. Slice the avocado into long sections and arrange around the crab meat. Add some freshly ground pepper and garnish with the lemon wedges.

When following the 30-Day Plan, we suggest you eat fresh fruit and/or low-fat yogurt as a dessert after most Main Meals. However, if you are having a special meal or entertaining friends, you may wish to make a dessert for the occasion. Here are some ideas for delicious desserts that are mouthwatering and easy to prepare, as well as being nutritious. Use the ingredients suggested or adapt the ideas using other fruits. Each recipe serves two people.

Summer Berry Salad
8 strawberries
100 g (4 oz) raspberries
100 g (4 oz) blueberries
1 orange
2 sprigs mint

Rinse the berries and juice the orange. Gently mix together the berries and arrange in individual dishes. Spoon the orange juice over the berries and garnish with a sprig of mint. Serve chilled.

Winter Fruit Salad
1 apple
1 pear
1 banana
4 semi-dried apricots
1 orange
5 ml (1 tsp) cinnamon
50 ml (2 oz) split almonds

Rinse or peel the apple and pear, and peel the banana. Cut the apple, pear, banana and apricots into small pieces, gently mix together and arrange in individual dishes. Juice the orange, mix the cinnamon with the orange juice and spoon over the fruit. Lightly toast the almonds. Allow them to cool, then scatter over the fruit.

Apricot Fool
8 small apricots
125 ml (5 fl oz) low-fat natural yogurt
5 ml (1 tsp) clear honey

Rinse the apricots and cut them in half. Poach the apricots lightly for 5 or 6 minutes in 75 ml (3 fl oz) water, stirring to prevent sticking. Reduce the liquid to 5 ml (1 tsp), then allow to cool. Stir in the honey and yogurt and mix thoroughly. Spoon into individual dishes. Serve chilled.

Caribbean Kebabs
½ mango
½ papaya
1 banana
wedge of pineapple
1 passion fruit

Peel the mango, papaya, banana and pineapple. Cut the fruit into bite-size pieces and arrange on wooden kebab sticks. Place the kebabs on serving plates. Cut the passion fruit in half and spoon the passion-fruit flesh over the kebabs. Serve chilled.

Eating out

When eating out in restaurants, choose foods that you enjoy but that are low in fat. Try to avoid eating vegetables covered in butter or sauces that are full of fat. Instead, select light but nutritious dishes. If you do eat more than usual, don't dwell on it too much or give up your new healthy lifestyle; simply return the next day to the healthy foods you have been eating and make sure you eat plenty of fresh fruit and vegetables. Fitting in a brisk 30-minute walk before dinner will burn away up to 200 calories and increase your metabolism, thus burning off even more calories.

When you've started to feel the benefits of fitness walking and healthy eating, you won't feel as inclined to overindulge, because you won't want to give up your feelings of renewed energy and vitality.

Shopping

Here are some lists of nutritious foods used in The Walker's Diet to help you when you go shopping.

Vegetables
onions (white, red, shallots, spring onions), garlic, carrots, broccoli, spinach, leeks, cabbage, cauliflower, parsnips, peas (petits pois), aubergines, mushrooms, peppers (red, green), courgettes, asparagus, sweetcorn, fennel, potatoes, sweet potatoes, celeriac, celery, beetroot, tomatoes, lettuce and other salad leaves, watercress, avocado, cucumber, chillis

Fruit
lemons, oranges, grapefruit, apples, bananas, pears, apricots, peaches, nectarines, mangoes, papayas, grapes, melon (cantaloupe, charentais, galia, honeydew, watermelon), pineapple,

passion fruit, kiwi fruit, strawberries, raspberries, blueberries, blackcurrants, redcurrants

Fish
cod, salmon, mackerel, herrings (fresh, roll mop), tuna, sword-fish, monkfish, sardines, scampi, prawns, squid, crab, smoked salmon, smoked trout, smoked mackerel

Meat
chicken breast fillets, turkey breast fillets, lean beef, lamb and pork, ham (cooked, Parma), bacon

Herbs and spices
basil, parsley, chives, sage, dill, mint, thyme, coriander, cumin, paprika, ginger, cinnamon

Nuts and seeds
almonds, brazil nuts, walnuts, pine nuts, cashew nuts, seeds (pumpkin, sesame, sunflower)

Groceries
rice (wholegrain, basmati), couscous, pasta (penne, bucatini, spaghetti), bread (wholemeal, pitta), soft tortillas, tuna (in water), lentils, chick peas, beans (red kidney, borlotti, cannellini, baked), tomatoes, tomato purée, chilli sauce, Nam Pla fish sauce, anchovies, capers, olives, mustard, creamed horseradish, dried apricots, prunes, sultanas, clear honey, ground almonds, eggs, low-fat natural yogurt, low-fat mayonnaise, cheese (feta, mozzarella, Parmesan, low-fat cottage), semi-skimmed milk, low-fat single cream, curry paste, olive oil, safflower oil (or other vegetable oil), balsamic vinegar, white wine vinegar, wine (red, white), sea salt, whole black pepper

- Think ahead: make sure you have plenty of fruit and vegetables available. It is very easy to give in to buying fast foods, which may not be as healthy.
- Take advantage of the fact that many shops and supermarkets now stock a varied selection of delicious fruits and vegetables from all over the world. Many of them tell you how to prepare these foods – if they don't, then ask.
- Give yourself treats: have delicious fruits for a dessert after your Main Meal. There's nothing so nice as fresh mango, melon or summer berries.

TIPS FOR HEALTHY EATING

- Follow the guidelines of the Healthy-Eating Pyramid
- Eat more fresh foods and less processed foods
- Eat more complex carbohydrates (see page 191) and less sugary and fatty foods, especially saturated fats (see page 193)
- Eat more grains, pulses, fish and white meat
- When buying red meat, choose lean cuts
- Whenever possible, eat wholefoods – foods that have not been processed or refined more than is necessary
- Eat foods when they are in season
- Read labels to find out the amount of saturated fat, etc
- If you are making changes to your diet, make them gradually
- Make sure you have a varied diet – and enjoy your food!

Superfoods for healthy snacks

- crudités – raw vegetables cut into bite-size pieces
- fresh fruit
- fresh fruit and vegetable juices
- dried fruit – apricots, prunes, etc

- unsalted nuts and raisins (not too many nuts as they have a high fat content)
- unsalted nuts – almonds, walnuts, brazil nuts, hazelnuts, pine nuts
- your own preferred mix of seeds – pumpkin, sesame, sunflower
- low-fat natural yogurt, with fresh fruit added if you wish
- small pitta bread with salad filling
- crispbread with sliced tomato

The healthy choice

- semi-skimmed milk instead of full-fat milk
- low-fat natural yogurt or low-fat single cream instead of full-fat cream
- olive oil instead of butter
- tomato- or yogurt-based sauces instead of cheese, cream or other full-fat sauces
- herbs or spices for flavouring instead of salt
- low-fat natural yogurt or fresh fruit for dessert instead of rich puddings
- fresh fruit and vegetable juices or water instead of coffee and tea
- fish or white meat instead of red meat
- lemon juice or low-fat mayonnaise instead of salad dressing or full-fat mayonnaise
- fresh fruit or crudités instead of sugary or fatty snacks

Walker's Diet Superfoods

Try and eat these superfoods at least once a week. You may find that you eat some of them almost every day.

spinach   broccoli   cabbage   onions   avocado
carrots   beans   tomatoes   peppers   parsley
apples   bananas   oranges   pink grapefruit   apricots   berries
eggs   sardines   salmon
low-fat natural yogurt   extra virgin olive oil
olives   oats   nuts   seeds

FURTHER FOOD FACTS FOR FITNESS WALKERS

This is a reference guide to the main nutrients: carbohydrates, protein, fat, vitamins, minerals and water.

Carbohydrates

Carbohydrates produce energy, and their rapid absorption means they are ideal fuel for exercise. According to the World Health Organisation, about half of each day's energy value should come from this nutrient. Carbohydrates are either simple (refined sugars) or complex (starches). Your aim each day should be to eat foods containing mainly complex carbohydrates.

simple carbohydrates
- pure or refined sugar providing energy but no other nutrients
- found in jam, honey, sweets and chocolates

complex carbohydrates
- starches usually found with other nutrients, such as vitamins and minerals
- found in bread, pasta, rice, oats, apples, bananas, dried fruits, potatoes, beans, lentils

Fibre

Fibre is unrefined carbohydrate, providing filling food without being fattening. It passes through the digestive tract without being completely broken down and helps food and waste products pass through the digestive system. Fibre is found in fruit and vegetables (particularly in the skins), nuts and pulses. By following the Healthy-Eating Pyramid and the recipes in the 30-Day Healthy-Eating Plan, you will be including plenty of fibre in your diet.

There are two types of fibre, soluble and insoluble. Soluble fibre is found in fruit and vegetables, seeds and oats. It is believed to help lower blood cholesterol levels and may decrease the incidence of heart disease. Insoluble fibre is found in whole grains and in the outer part of fruit and vegetables. It promotes more efficient elimination of body waste and may help to relieve some digestive disorders. In processed foods, the outer part of fruits and vegetables is usually removed. Another good reason for eating fresh foods rather than processed foods!

Protein

Protein is required for energy, growth and renewal. The body needs many forms of protein for the structure and repair of cells, and also to form hormones and enzymes. However, most Westerners eat more protein than is actually necessary and the body stores the excess as fat.

high-quality proteins: fish, meat, poultry, soya beans, eggs

low-quality proteins: bread, potatoes, pasta, rice, nuts

Fat

Fat is an essential part of our diet, supplying concentrated energy. The brain, muscles, heart, hair, skin and immune system, among other things, all need fat in order to function effectively. Saturated fats are usually solid at room temperature and come mainly from animal sources, such as butter and lard. Unsaturated fats are usually liquid at room temperature. They include most vegetable oils, such as olive oil, which is high in monounsaturated fatty acids, and safflower, sunflower and corn oil, which are high in polyunsaturated fatty acids.

A unique kind of polyunsaturated fatty acid, called omega-3, is found in oily fish, and is linked to a reduced risk of heart disease. Studies show that there is almost no record of heart disease among Greenland Eskimos, who eat large amounts of this kind of fish.

Meat, poultry and fish can be steamed, grilled, baked or roasted on a rack to reduce fat content.

A healthy balance of fats

Eat more of:
foods rich in omega-3 polyunsaturated fatty acids, such as oily fish, including herrings, mackerel, sardines, kippers, salmon, tuna

Eat small amounts of:
foods rich in omega-6 polyunsaturated fatty acids, such as sunflower seeds and oil, and walnuts

Eat less:
foods rich in saturated and trans fatty acids, such as dairy fats and solid fats

Vitamins and minerals

It is important to eat a varied diet of high-nutrient foods to obtain the vitamins and minerals necessary for good health and vitality. A shortage of nutrients, which can cause poor health, is mainly due to poor eating habits, such as eating too few vegetables and fruit, too much processed food, too many fatty or sugary foods or drinking too much alcohol. Vitamin and mineral supplements can help, but they are not a good substitute for eating healthily.

Vitamins are either water-soluble or fat-soluble. Water-soluble vitamins are the B group and vitamin C. They cannot be stored in the body and therefore need to be replaced every day.

- The B vitamins give protection against infection, help in energy production, promote growth and are necessary for a healthy nervous system. They can be found in foods such as wholemeal bread, nuts, brown rice, pulses, meat, fish, eggs, green vegetables, bananas and cheese.
- Vitamin C is used in the growth and repair of cells, gums, bones, teeth and blood vessels and helps in the healing of disease. It can be found in green leafy vegetables, potatoes, tomatoes, berries and other fruits, especially citrus fruits.

The fat-soluble vitamins, A, D, E and K, can be stored. They are necessary for various bodily functions, including giving protection against infection and helping to promote growth.

- Vitamin A helps in the maintenance of healthy growth and development. It can be found in liver, carrots, dark-green leafy vegetables and orange-coloured fruits such as apricots, peaches and cantaloupe melon.
- Vitamin D is necessary for healthy bones and teeth. It is found in eggs and fish oils, and can be manufactured by the body when exposed to sunshine.
- Vitamin E is a natural antioxidant (see page 199) and is vital for the production of red blood cells. It can be found in eggs, nuts, leafy vegetables and vegetable oils.

- Vitamin K helps maintain healthy blood and the functioning of some bone and kidney proteins. It is found in meat, leafy vegetables and soya beans.

Minerals help build bones, carry nerve signals and clot blood. Key minerals such as calcium, iron, zinc, potassium, magnesium and selenium can be found in green vegetables, potatoes, beans, citrus fruits, apples, bananas, nuts, seeds, oat bran, milk, cheese, seafood, poultry, meat and eggs.

Water

Water is the body's most important nutrient. See pages 42–43 in the 30-Day Walking Workout for facts about water.

The following information will help you maintain a healthy, balanced diet.

Cut down on processed foods

If you are buying processed foods, look carefully at the labels. Some foods seem to be low in fat but are actually surprisingly high in fat. Or a food may sound healthy, but when you see the label, you realise how little goodness there really is in it. Remember, as a general rule, fresh is best. And look out on labels for words indicating that a product contains hidden sugar, salt and fat. Here are some examples:

- sugar: sucrose, dextrose, syrup, concentrated fruit juice, hydrogenated glucose syrup
- salt: sodium chloride, bicarbonate of soda, monosodium glutamate
- fat: hydrogenated vegetable fat, full-fat milk powder, palm or coconut oil

Fresh fruit and vegetable juices

Fresh fruit and vegetables not only look good and taste good – they do us a power of good too. One delicious way of benefiting from these life-enhancing wonderfoods is to juice them raw and literally drink their goodness to give you an instant energy boost. All you need is a juicer. There is now a good choice of juicing machines available in the shops at a moderate price.

But what about 'freshly squeezed' juices from the supermarket? Let's compare facts. The so-called 'freshly squeezed' juices have actually been in the bottle for some time, thus losing some of their vitamin content. The price of bought juices is considerable; you could soon have paid for a juicer if you regularly bought ready-made juices instead. You have complete freedom of choice if you juice your own fruit and vegetables. And there is no comparison between the taste of a fresh and a bought juice.

An excellent combination to start with is carrot and apple. It is difficult to give exact quantities for juices as, for example, some carrots are juicier than others. If you make your own juices regularly, you will soon find the right quantities. But for one person, try juicing 4 medium carrots and 1 large apple. Wash the fruit and vegetables and trim where necessary. Then simply juice them and enjoy a glass of instant energy.

Carrot juice is a good base to which you can add any other fruit and vegetable juices. Here are some suggestions: carrot, apple, pineapple, melon, grape, pear, kiwi fruit, mango, tomato, beetroot, celery, cucumber, spinach, watercress, red and green pepper. Try different combinations and make a note of the ones you particularly enjoy. And add a little basil, parsley or ginger for a subtle difference.

It's always best to buy foods when they are in season, and this rule should also be applied when making your choice for juices. Not only do fruit and vegetables taste better when they are in season, they are also much cheaper.

Salt

Sodium chloride, or table salt, not only enhances the flavour of food, it is also a preservative. Sodium is an essential mineral, but, although the daily requirement is different for each person, the amount we need is quite small. Westerners generally consume too much salt, partly through eating fast food, which is usually over-salted, but also through eating freshly cooked foods that have had too much salt added to them.

Eating too much salt has been associated with hypertension, but the connection is not clearly understood. However, many people wish to reduce their intake of salt and the best way to do so is to cut down gradually. In this way, you will not crave salty foods and you will soon become accustomed to foods that are not so highly salted. Also try using other flavourings in your cooking, such as herbs and spices.

Herbs and spices

Try making herbs and spices a part of everyday food preparation – their use subtly enhances the flavour of food, and many of them provide excellent health benefits. There is a huge variety of both herbs and spices widely available. When possible, use fresh herbs, which are easy to grow in the garden or on a windowsill. If you are not able to grow your own, most supermarkets now stock fresh herbs and shops often indicate to which foods the herbs are particularly suited. If the quantity in which they are sold is too great, then freeze them. Cut or tear the herb into pieces, then put into an ice-cube tray and top up with water. When the herb cubes are frozen, they can be put into a freezer bag and used as required. Simply defrost, drain the water and add the herb to your food. Try using basil, parsley, chives, sage, dill, mint, thyme and any others you like or would like to try.

When choosing spices, buy them in fairly small quantities and store in a dark place, as they soon lose their freshness. It is worth making the effort to grind your own whole spices, in a pestle and mortar or a coffee grinder, as both the aroma and taste are wonderful.

Tea and coffee

The caffeine content of these drinks varies considerably, depending on the product and how it is prepared. However, as a general rule, a cup of tea contains half to two-thirds as much caffeine as a cup of coffee, green tea normally contains less caffeine than black tea, and loose tea leaves contain less caffeine than the same brand made from a tea bag. Studies show that tea, particularly green tea, contains powerful antioxidants to help prevent heart disease and cancer.

There is no evidence that caffeine will do any harm to a healthy adult who drinks tea and coffee in moderation. But if you feel that you drink too much tea and coffee, or if you wish to drink less for your general well-being, then cut down gradually. This way, you should avoid side effects such as headaches or feelings of irritability. You could try decaffeinated drinks or simply start to enjoy drinking more water or fresh fruit and vegetable juices.

Alcohol

Evidence suggests that consuming small amounts of any form of alcohol can help reduce the risk of death from a stroke. Red wine, in particular, contains antioxidants, and taken in moderation – one or two glasses daily – can help protect against heart disease. However, these benefits need to be balanced against the negative effects of alcohol. Alcohol is more destructive of nutrients than any other commonly consumed substance. It can deplete the body of B vitamins, folic acid, vitamin C, zinc, magnesium, and potassium, all of which are required for health and vitality and to maintain the body's immune defence mechanism. Alcohol also dehydrates the body.

If you want to cut down on alcohol, you could avoid alcoholic drinks before a meal by drinking mineral water with ice and lemon. Or try drinking a spritzer – half a glass of wine topped up with soda water. And when you pour your own drinks, have a smaller glass of wine than usual and drink equal amounts of water to avoid dehydration.

Antioxidants

Antioxidants are thought to protect the body against some diseases by preventing the harmful reactions of free radicals. Although free radicals are used by the body, among other things to defend against invasive bacteria, they can, if overproduced, cause damage to cells. Antioxidants are also thought to help strengthen the immune system and fight infection generally.

Here are some of the main sources of antioxidant vitamins and minerals:

- beta-carotene (the pigment in many fruit and vegetables which is converted to vitamin A) – carrots, dark-green leafy vegetables and orange-coloured fruits
- vitamin C – fresh fruits, particularly citrus fruits, and vegetables
- vitamin E – vegetable oils, leafy vegetables, eggs, nuts
- selenium – fish, chicken, bread, kidneys, vegetables
- manganese – wholegrain cereals, pulses, beans, green leafy vegetables, bananas, nuts, tea

Cholesterol

Cholesterol is manufactured by the body; it is an essential part of the blood and it is found in all body cells. It is also found in all animal foods except egg white. The connection between cholesterol in the blood and that in foods is not certain, but it is thought that an excessive amount of cholesterol in the blood is associated with heart disease. Foods which are high in cholesterol include eggs, kidneys, liver, and some shellfish, such as prawns and lobster. But it is generally thought that foods that are high in saturated fat help raise the blood cholesterol level, rather than foods that contain high amounts of cholesterol but are low in fat, such as prawns.

Cholesterol is carried in the bloodstream by lipoproteins, of which there are two types, high-density lipoprotein (HDL) and low-density lipoprotein (LDL). HDL is protective and is sometimes known as 'good' cholesterol, but LDL encourages cholesterol to accumulate in the arteries and is therefore known as 'bad' cholesterol. The best ways to lower high blood cholesterol levels and to boost HDLs are to eat less saturated fat, stop smoking (if applicable), and take more exercise, such as fitness walking.

STEP IT OUT TO A LONGER LIFE

Now you've seen how easy it can be to step up your energy levels, get fit and stay healthy. And you've learned how to greet each day with enthusiasm and a feeling of confidence. As you will have proved to yourself, it really can be as simple as walking out of your own front door. All you have to do now is stay on track by following the simple guidelines in this book. They worked for us and we are sure they will work for you.